Graphic History of Architecture

JOHN MANSBRIDGE

Hennessey + Ingalls
Art + Architecture Books
Santa Monica 1999

Published in 1999
Hennessey + Ingalls
1254 3rd Street Promenade
Santa Monica, CA 90401

ISBN 0-940512-15-7

Manufactured in the United States of America.

Library of Congress Cataloging-in-Publication Data

Mansbridge, John
    Graphic history of architecture / John Mansbridge.
        p.   cm.
    Originally published: New York : Viking Press, 1967.
    Includes bibliographical references and index.
    ISBN 0-940512-15-7 (paper)
    1. Architecture--History--Outlines, syllabi, etc.   I. Title.
NA203.M26   1999
720' .9--dc21   98-49277

Preface

This work is designed as a *visual* textbook for students and as an introduction and guide for the general reader. Certain omissions have necessarily had to be made because of the vastness of the subject, but author, publisher and printer have done everything possible to make both the format and the reproductions clear and vivid.

Drawings and diagrams have been used in preference to photographs in order to give as clear a picture as possible of the three-dimensional form and the construction of buildings. Particular use has been made of drawings spread across facing pages : these double spreads, with comparative plans and elevations (drawn to the same scale whenever possible), show the transition from one style to another, for example from Romanesque to Perpendicular Gothic or from Renaissance to Baroque. (Scales or buildings are given in English feet, e.g. $\longmapsto\!\!\longrightarrow$ 20.)

Brief introductions, with maps and time-charts, indicate the historical backgrounds which have generated the need for specific kinds of buildings ; similarly attention is paid to the materials available, which determines the nature and final form of each construction.

In the preparation of this volume I have received assistance of one kind or another from so many people, not least from my students over the years, that it would be invidious, were it not impossible, to attempt to mention them all individually. But I should like to take this opportunity of acknowledging my considerable debt to Choisy, whose magnificent drawings have formed the basis of my own work ; I also want to thank especially Brian Batsford for his initial enthusiasm for the project, Peter Kemmis Betty for his patient editing and many helpful suggestions, and finally Mary Elizabeth Scaping. Not only did she provide great assistance with the lettering of the drawings, but without her constant encouragement the work would never have been completed. To her the book is dedicated.

Forest Hill
January 1967

John Mansbridge

Contents

4

Index

1 Places and Buildings

EGYPT

THE ARCHAIC PERIOD		THE OLD KINGDOM				First Inter-mediate Period	THE MIDDLE KINGDOM		Second Inter-mediate Period
Dynasty I	II	III	IV	V	VI		IX	XII	
c.3200 B.C. 2980	2789	2680	2565	2420		2258 2134	1991	1786	157
Union of Upper and Lower Egypt Capital: Heliopolis		Capital: Memphis The Age of the Pyramids					The Feudal Age Capital: Thebes		Invasion of the Hyksos from Asia

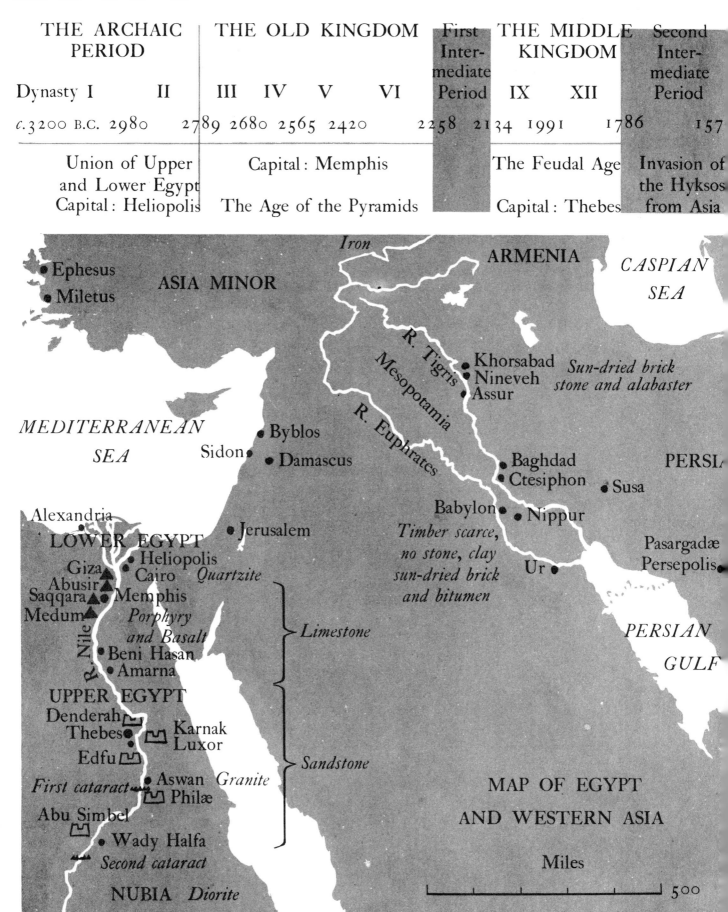

MAP OF EGYPT

AND WESTERN ASIA

Miles

500

INTRODUCTION

THE NEW KINGDOM				THE LATE PERIOD				THE PTOLEMAIC PERIOD
XVIII	XIX	XX		XXI	-	XXXI		
570	1314	1197	1085		671-663	525	332	30 B.C.
The Egyptian Empire in Asia and Nubia Capital: Thebes					Assyrian invasion	Domination of Persia		Egypt a Roman province

Egypt was a narrow strip of highly productive soil, 8 to 12 miles wide, along the banks of the Nile, about one-fifth of the area of England and Wales. From pre-dynastic times sun-dried mud bricks were used for houses, but these have not survived: timber was scarce and hence arches were built without centering. There was however an abundance of limestone, sandstone and granite. The planning of irrigation canals and fields, necessitated by the annual inundations of the Nile, demanded a system of geometry (Gk land measuring). Believing in a life after death, the Egyptians thought that the body should be preserved in a lasting tomb; this became a geometric construction of great solidity and permanence.

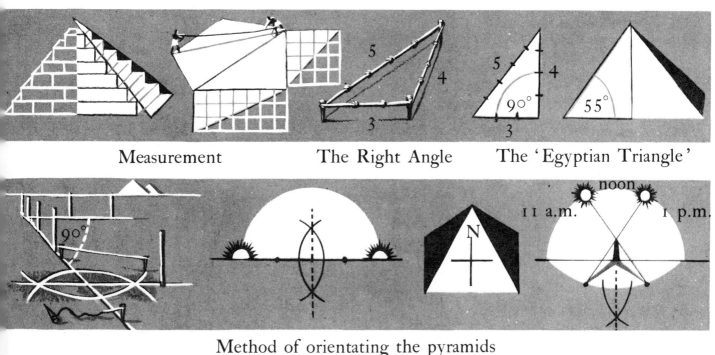

Measurement   The Right Angle   The 'Egyptian Triangle'

Method of orientating the pyramids

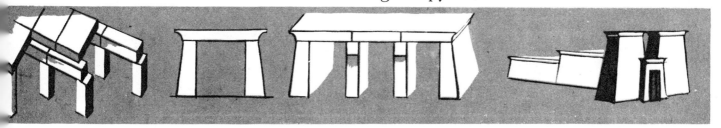

Temples constructed with columns, beams and massive, battered external walls

EGYPT

Pit graves in desert cemetries: sand heap A surrounded by circle of stones B over grave C

Pit graves transformed into tombs by brick lining and flat wooden or arched brick roofs

Walls of sun-dried brick

Beginning of *stone* masonry

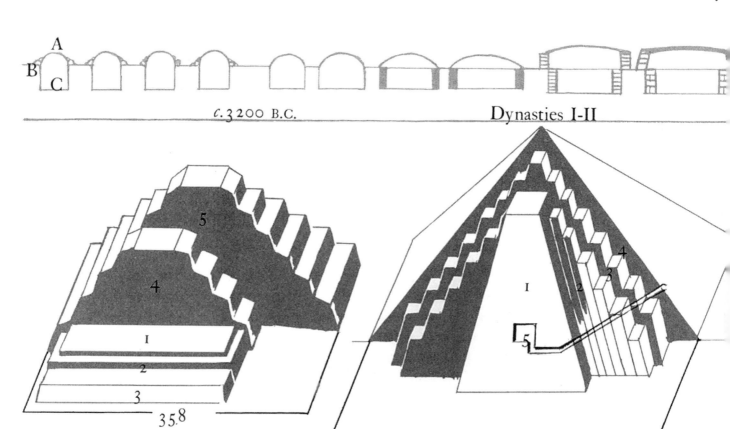

A
B
C

*c.*3200 B.C.   Dynasties I-II

35.8

473

THE STEP PYRAMID, Saqqara, Dynasty III : Section looking west Built by Imhotep, architect to King Zoser.

1 Begun as a mastaba-tomb. 2-5 Then successively enlarged, in limestone. Set within a complex of buildings (p.18)

THE PYRAMID OF MEDUM, Dynasties III-I Section looking west, reconstructed

1 Centre core. 2 Successive layers added, at abou 75°, each of local stone and cased with limestone 3 Enlargement of the pyramid. 4 Steps filled in with a facing of limestone. 5 The tomb chambe

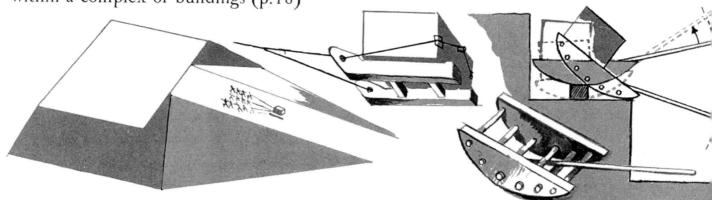

Stones on sledges. pulled up long earth ramps   The Rocker;   pulleys were unknow

Suggested methods of hauling and lifting stones

PYRAMIDS

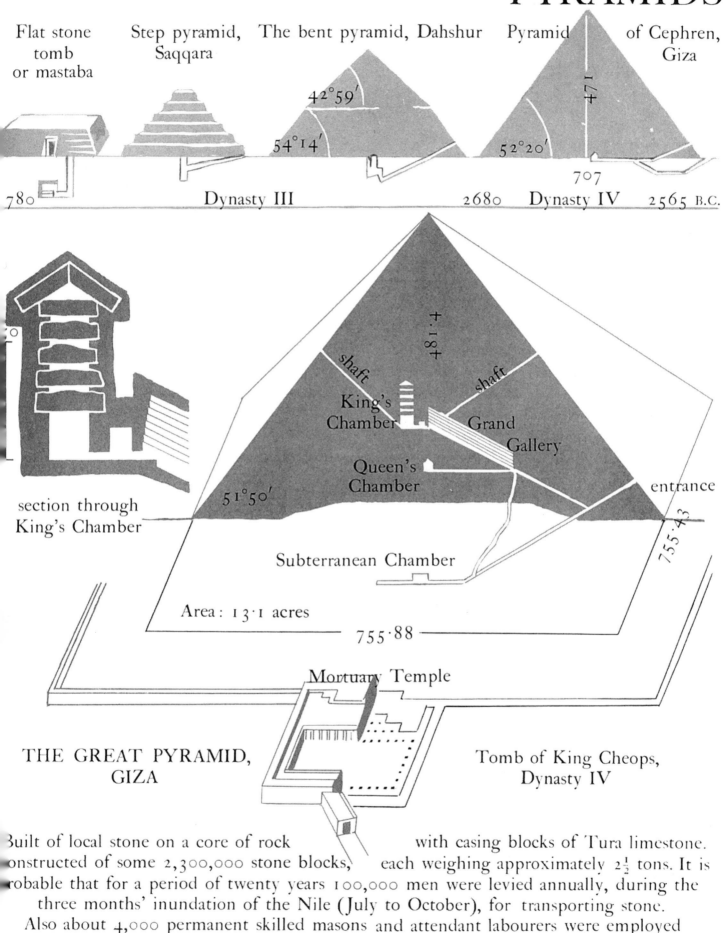

Flat stone tomb or mastaba

Step pyramid, Saqqara

The bent pyramid, Dahshur

Pyramid of Cephren, Giza

42°59′

54°14′

47¹

52°20′

7°7

780   Dynasty III   2680   Dynasty IV   2565 B.C.

481·4

shaft   shaft

King's Chamber

Grand Gallery

Queen's Chamber

51°50′

entrance

755·43

Subterranean Chamber

section through King's Chamber

Area : 13·1 acres

755·88

Mortuary Temple

THE GREAT PYRAMID, GIZA

Tomb of King Cheops, Dynasty IV

Built of local stone on a core of rock with casing blocks of Tura limestone. Constructed of some 2,300,000 stone blocks, each weighing approximately 2½ tons. It is probable that for a period of twenty years 100,000 men were levied annually, during the three months' inundation of the Nile (July to October), for transporting stone. Also about 4,000 permanent skilled masons and attendant labourers were employed

EGYPT

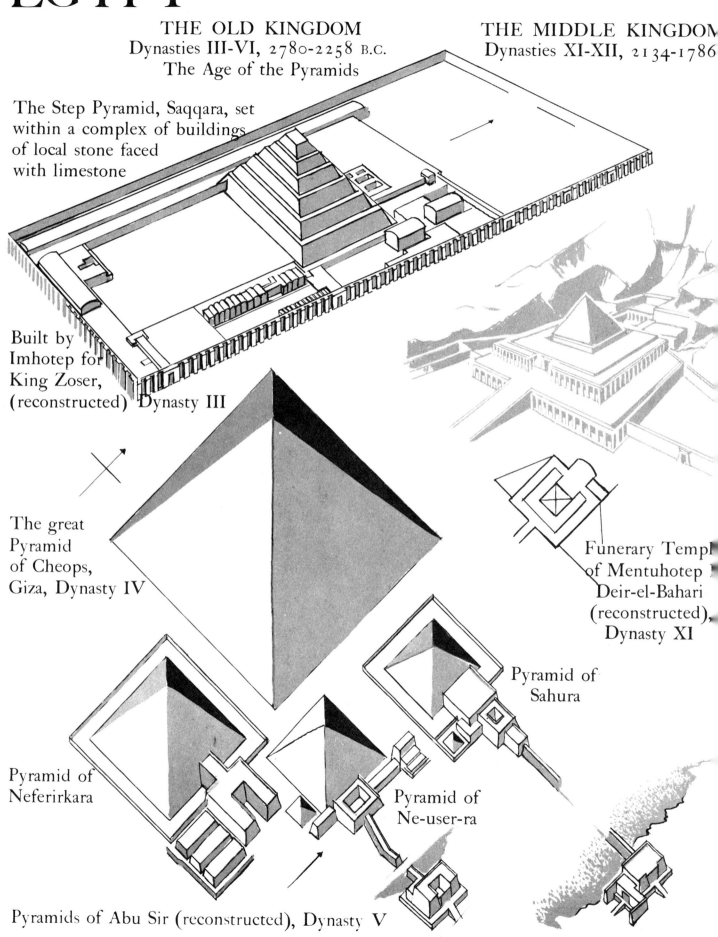

The Step Pyramid, Saqqara, set
within a complex of buildings
of local stone faced
with limestone

Built by
Imhotep for
King Zoser,
(reconstructed) Dynasty III

The great
Pyramid
of Cheops,
Giza, Dynasty IV

Funerary Templ
of Mentuhotep
Deir-el-Bahari
(reconstructed),
Dynasty XI

Pyramid of
Sahura

Pyramid of
Neferirkara

Pyramid of
Ne-user-ra

Pyramids of Abu Sir (reconstructed), Dynasty V

18

COMPARATIVE BUILDINGS & PLANS

THE NEW KINGDOM
Dynasties XVIII-XX, 1570-1085 B.C.
The Age of the great Temples

THE PTOLEMAIC PERIOD
332-30 B.C.
Revival of Temples

Mortuary Temple of Amon,
Deir-el-Bahari (reconstructed),
Dynasty XVIII
Designed by Senmut and
built for Queen Hatshepsut

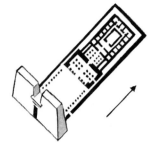

The Temple of Horus,
Edfu, 237-212 B.C.
Begun by Ptolemy III

The Great Temple
of Amon, Karnak,
Dynasties XVIII-XXXI
(Foundations Dynasty XI)

The Temple
of Amon, Luxor,
Dynasties XVIII-XIX
Begun by Amenhotep III
and added to by Rameses II

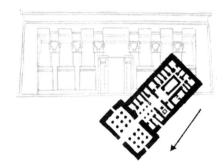

The Temple of Hathor,
Dendera, 1st cent. B.C.

Temple of Seti I, Abydos,
Dynasty XIX

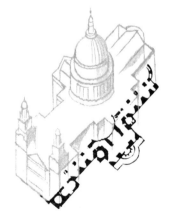

St Paul's, London

Great Temple, Abu Simbel, Nubia,
Dynasty XIX. Built for Rameses II

Plans and buildings in black
drawn to the same scale

500

EGYPT

THE TEMPLE OF KHONSU, KARNAK

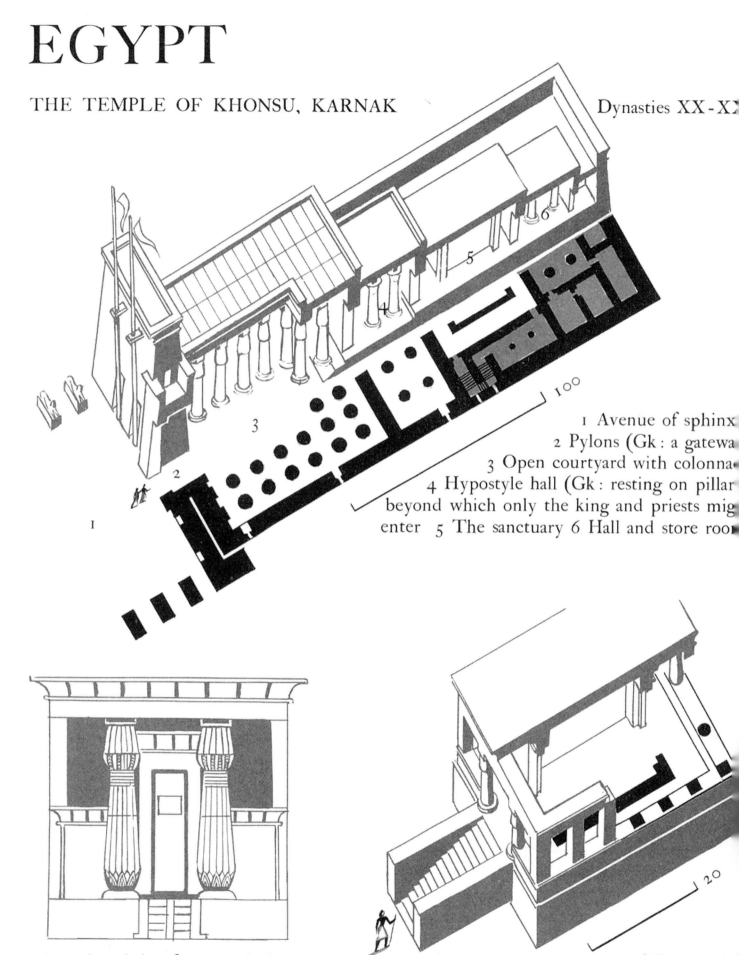

1 Avenue of sphinx
2 Pylons (Gk: a gatewa
3 Open courtyard with colonna
4 Hypostyle hall (Gk: resting on pillar
beyond which only the king and priests mig
enter 5 The sanctuary 6 Hall and store roo

A garden shrine from a painting
in a tomb, Thebes, Dynasty XIX

Temple of Amenhotep III, Island of Elephanti
Dynasty XVIII   (Destroyed A.D. 1822)

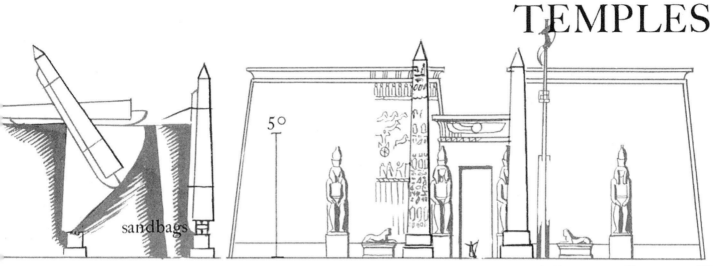

sandbags

Pylons, Temple of Luxor, Dynasty XIX. Built by Rameses II

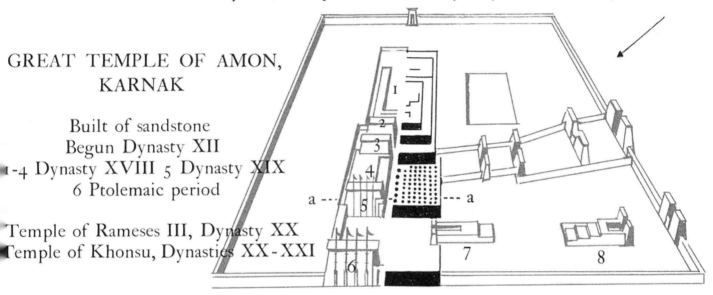

GREAT TEMPLE OF AMON, KARNAK

Built of sandstone
Begun Dynasty XII
1-4 Dynasty XVIII 5 Dynasty XIX
6 Ptolemaic period

Temple of Rameses III, Dynasty XX
Temple of Khonsu, Dynasties XX - XXI

Section

Hypostyle hall, a-a

clerestory windows

hall filled with sand
and roof-slabs lowered
into position

EGYPT

Valley Temple
built of granite:
Pyramid of Cephren, Giza.

Dynasty IV

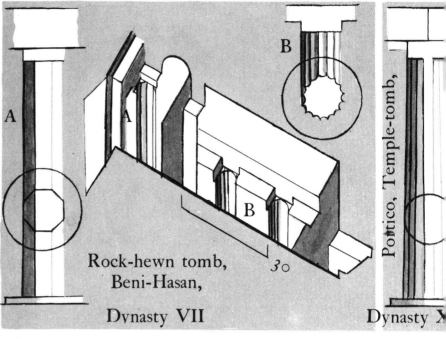

A

B

Rock-hewn tomb,
Beni-Hasan,

30

Dynasty VII

Portico, Temple-tomb,

Dynasty X

COLUMN & BEAM

PROTO-DORIC COLUMNS

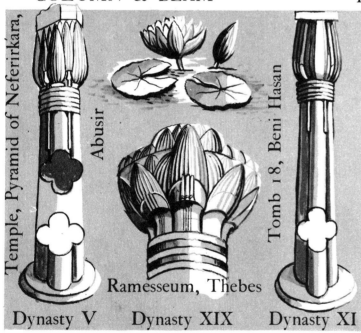

Temple, Pyramid of Neferirkára,
Abusir

Ramesseum, Thebes

Tomb 18, Beni Hasan

Dynasty V   Dynasty XIX   Dynasty XI

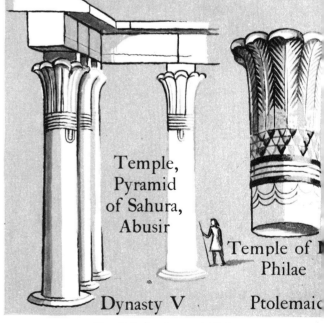

Temple,
Pyramid
of Sahura,
Abusir

Temple of
Philae

Dynasty V   Ptolemaic

LOTUS COLUMNS

PALM COLUMNS

gorge
cornice

palm
branches

roll moulding

bundle of reeds

Brick arch,
el 'Asaseef, Thebes

Vault of damp mud bricks laid
slanted courses without centering

COLUMN BEAM & ARCH

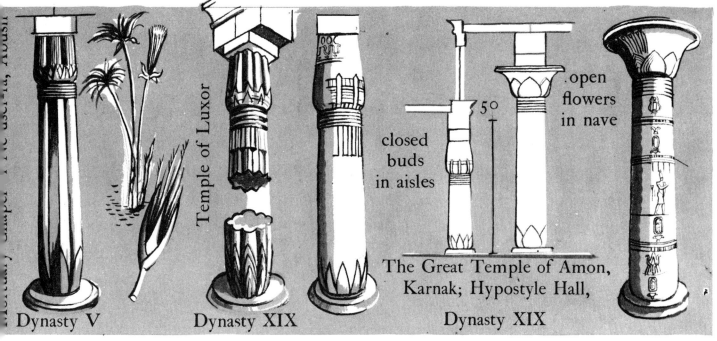

Temple of Luxor

closed buds in aisles

5o

open flowers in nave

The Great Temple of Amon, Karnak; Hypostyle Hall,

Dynasty V   Dynasty XIX   Dynasty XIX

PAPYRUS COLUMNS

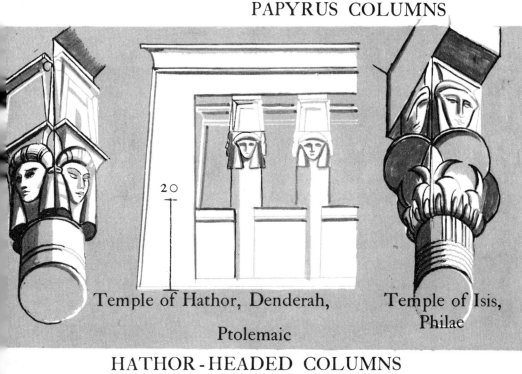

2o

Temple of Hathor, Denderah,

Ptolemaic

Temple of Isis, Philae

Ptolemaic

HATHOR-HEADED COLUMNS   COMPOSITE

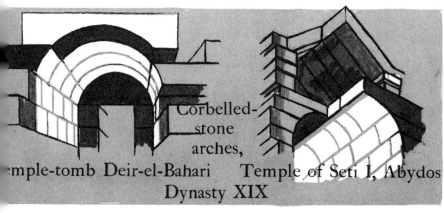

Corbelled-stone arches,

mple-tomb Deir-el-Bahari   Temple of Seti I, Abydos

Dynasty XIX

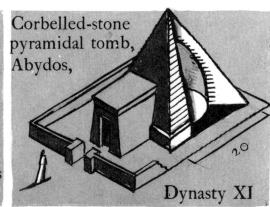

Corbelled-stone pyramidal tomb, Abydos,

2o

Dynasty XI

WESTERN ASIA

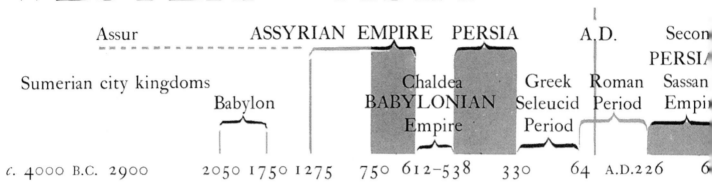

Assur			ASSYRIAN EMPIRE	PERSIA		A.D.		Secon
								PERSIA
Sumerian city kingdoms				Chaldea	Greek	Roman	Sassan	
				BABYLONIAN	Seleucid	Period	Empi	
	Babylon			Empire	Period			
c. 4000 B.C. 2900	2050 1750 1275		750	612-538	330	64	A.D.226	6

SUMERIAN CITY KINGDOMS

Civilization in Western Asia began with city kingdoms in the rich alluvial plain between t
lower Tigris and the Euphrates, an area about that of Wales (Map p. 14).   Tower-temp
or ziggurats were the centre of city life.   There was no stone and little timber but clay v
moulded into sun-dried brick. Buildings were faced with kiln-baked bricks, sparingly owi
to lack of fuel.

ASSYRIA

Assyria was set on a high tableland of lime-stone, harder rock & alabaster, but the Assyri
continued to use sun-dried and kiln-baked bricks. Palaces of warrior-kings were built on la
platforms of brick 30-50 feet high. Lower courses of walls were faced with slabs of alabas
9-12 feet high and carved with bas-reliefs or covered with plaster and painted with brig
colour.   The arch was constructed for gateways, vaults and drains.

SECOND BABYLONIAN EMPIRE

Nebuchadnezzar (604-561 B.C.) rebuilt Babylon to a regular plan described in *The Histor*
by Herodotus (484-406 B.C.). Buildings were of kiln-baked brick and bitumen.

PERSIAN EMPIRE

Palaces were built at the capital city of Susa, at Pasargadae and Persepolis, being construc
of stone which was abundant in Persia; whilst raised platforms and glazed coloured bric
were adapted from the Assyrians; also influences from Babylon, Syria and Egypt.

SECOND PERSIAN—SASSANID—EMPIRE

The capital city at Ctesiphon.   Buildings were erected of kiln-baked brick, vaults and th
earliest domes being built over square compartments, developed by the Byzantines.

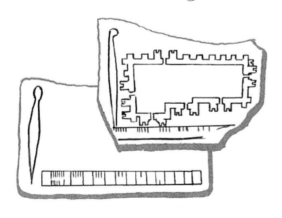

Stilus, scale and plan of
King Gudea of Lagash, c.2350 B.C.

The Ziggurat, Ur (restored), c.2350 B.C.

24

INTRODUCTION - ASSYRIA

Ziggurat, or temple observatory

South-east gateway A

PALACE
OF SAGON II
KHORSABAD
(restored)
772-705 B.C.

Both the platform,
about 50 ft high and
25 acres in extent, and
the palace built of sun-
dried brick and faced
with kiln-baked brick

Brick drain   under palace
built without centering

WESTERN ASIA BABYLON

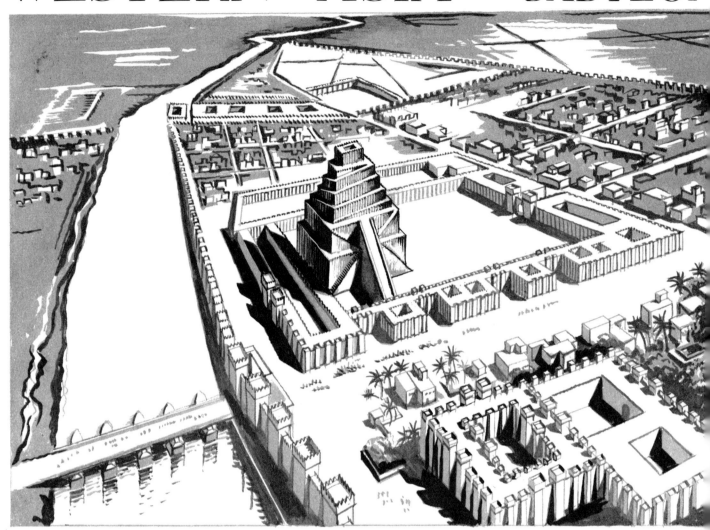

THE CITY OF BABYLON
(reconstructed),
as rebuilt by Nebuchadnezzar,
604-561 B.C., during the Second
Babylonian Empire.
Described in *The Histories* of Herodotus

House with roof-garden

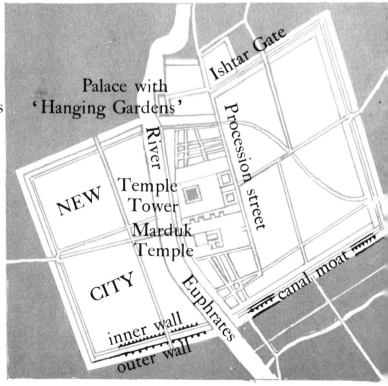

Palace with
'Hanging Gardens'

Ishtar Gate

Procession street

River

NEW

Temple
Tower

Marduk
Temple

CITY

Euphrates

canal moat

inner wall

outer wall

PERSIA

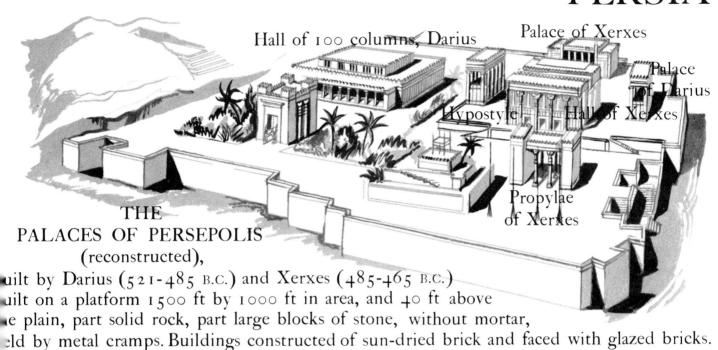

Hall of 100 columns, Darius
Palace of Xerxes
Palace of Darius
Hypostyle
Hall of Xerxes
Propylae of Xerxes

THE
PALACES OF PERSEPOLIS
(reconstructed),
Built by Darius (521-485 B.C.) and Xerxes (485-465 B.C.)
Built on a platform 1500 ft by 1000 ft in area, and 40 ft above
the plain, part solid rock, part large blocks of stone, without mortar,
held by metal cramps. Buildings constructed of sun-dried brick and faced with glazed bricks.
Columns of stone and flat roofs of cedar wood

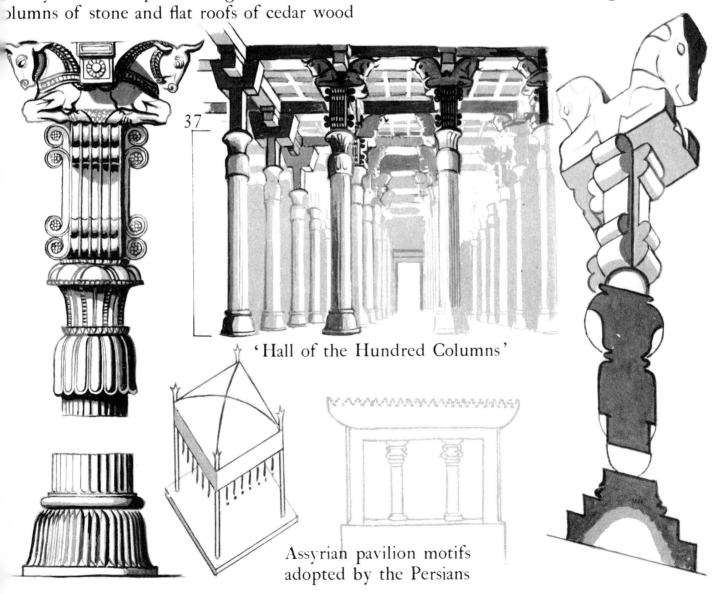

37

'Hall of the Hundred Columns'

Assyrian pavilion motifs
adopted by the Persians

WESTERN ASIA VAULTS &

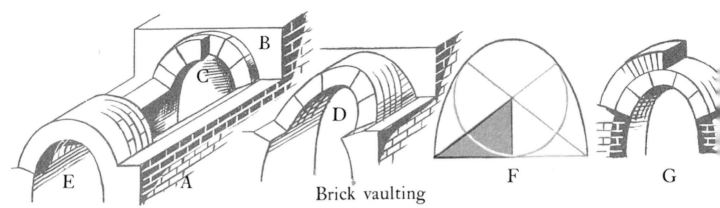

Brick vaulting

Bricks were laid to form a base A; against an end wall B wedge-shaped bricks were fix
with mortar C. To ensure adherence these were often laid in sloping courses D. An ar
was constructed with little or no centering to complete the vault E. To facilitate work a
to reduce pressure, vaults (and domes) had a high oval profile F. When completed vau
were often re-inforced by a second or more courses of brick G. Sassanid Persian buildin
vaults and domes were constructed of kiln-baked bricks laid with a mortar of lime and sa

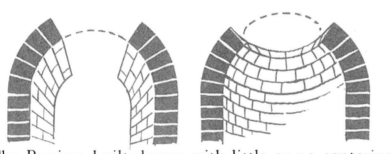

The Persians built domes with little or no centering.
A dome is an arched construction both vertically &
horizontally: each ring of brick or stone once closed
in cannot fall if it rests adequately on the ring below

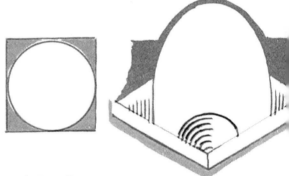

The Persians were the first to ere
circular domes on square plans w
four angular corbelled semi-dom

The Palace, Serbistan (exterior restored), *c.* A.D. 350

50

28

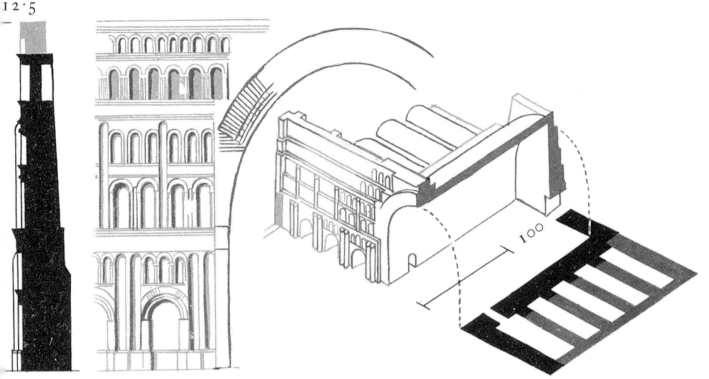

The Palace of Chosroes, Ctesiphon, 6th cent. A.D.

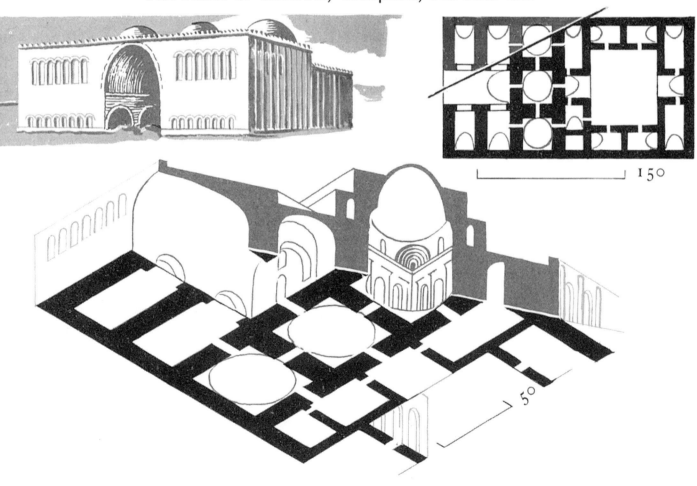

The Palace, Firouzabad (exterior restored), c. A.D. 450

GREEK

AEGEAN

c.2500 B.C. — 1184

Minoan—Crete

1500 — 1184

Mycenaean

HELLENI

775/6 First Olympiad

650 — 5

Archaic period

Establishment of Greek city-states along the Mediterranean and Black Sea

c.835 Homer

c.582 Pythagoras c.5

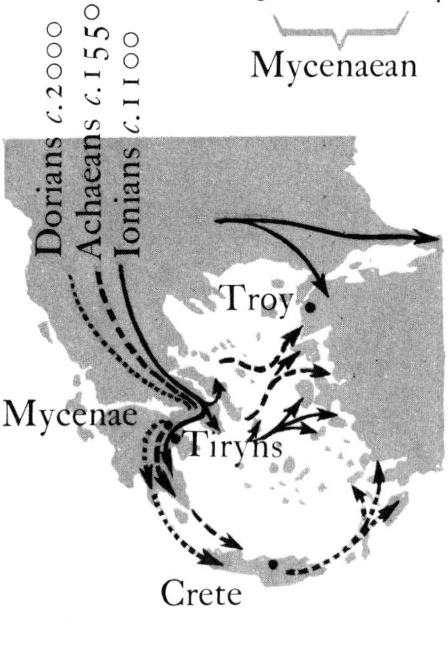

Dorians c.2000
Achaeans c.1550
Ionians c.1100
Troy
Mycenae
Tiryns
Crete

The Greek invasions

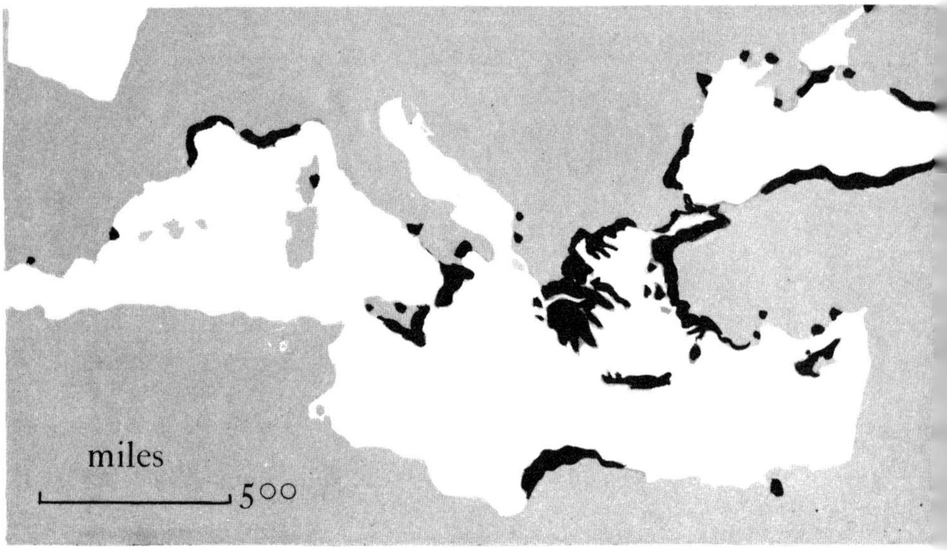

miles
500

Greek colonisation 8th-6th centuries B.C.

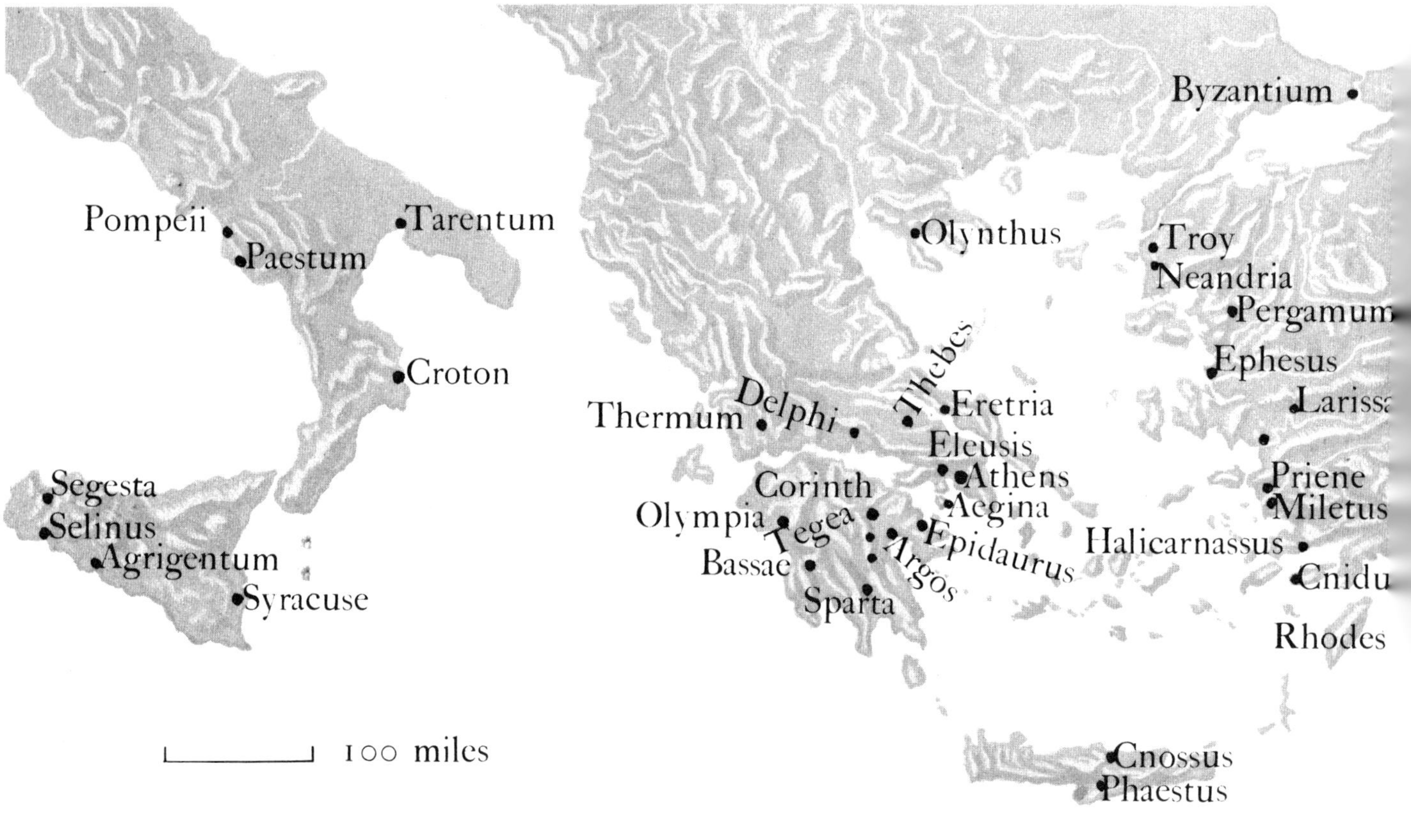

Byzantium
Pompeii
Paestum
Tarentum
Olynthus
Troy
Neandria
Pergamum
Ephesus
Croton
Thebes
Delphi
Thermum
Eretria
Larissa
Eleusis
Athens
Priene
Miletus
Segesta
Corinth
Aegina
Olympia
Tegea
Epidaurus
Halicarnassus
Selinus
Argos
Agrigentum
Bassae
Cnidu
Syracuse
Sparta
Rhodes
100 miles
Cnossus
Phaestus

INTRODUCTION

HELLENISTIC

2-479 444-429   334—323   146   31 B.C.
War   Ascendancy   Alexander the Great   Greece
ith   of Athens   King of Macedon   a Roman
rsia   431 — 404   province
        Peloponnesian War   323 Euclid 283
            429/8 Plato 347
              384 Aristotle 332

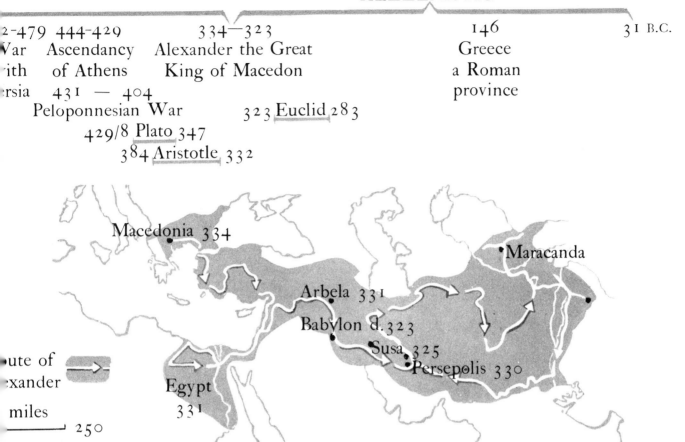

ute of
xander

miles
————— 250

Macedonia 334
·Maracanda
Arbela 331
Babylon d. 323
Susa 325
Persepolis 330
Egypt
331

The Empire of Alexander the Great

e Aegean Period. 1 No records survive of the Minoan sea-kings of Crete except remains
palaces, e.g. Cnossus. 2 The Mycenaeans built massive citadels with Cyclopean masonry
    and domed tholos tombs on the mainland. The Aegean civilization
                    fell before the Homeric Greeks.
e Hellenic Period. The Greeks called themselves Hellenes (Hellas was called Graecia by
Romans). They formed numerous small city states in which primitive houses surrounded
tadel and later a temple built on an acropolis or upper city. National unity was achieved
by pan-Hellenic festivals held at Olympia, Delphi, Argos and Corinth every few years.
e Hellenistic Period began with the Empire created by Alexander the Great when many
            new cities were founded with monumental buildings.
e Greek temple developed from the Mycenaean megaron built of sun-dried brick, stone
timber to house a deity and to be looked at from outside, not to contain a congregation
nin. The arch was known to the Greeks, but they based their temples on the column &
n. These developed from the 6th-4th centuries B.C., each with its own ratios of proport-
established by experience. Columns were often placed closer than necessary to support
entablature in order to create a repetitive rhythm of solids and voids. Optical refinements
playing an appearance of vitality and strength have been measured in a number of them.
ny architects wrote treatises about their buildings, cited by Vitruvius (1st cent. B.C.) who
                classified their plans and proportions.

GREEK

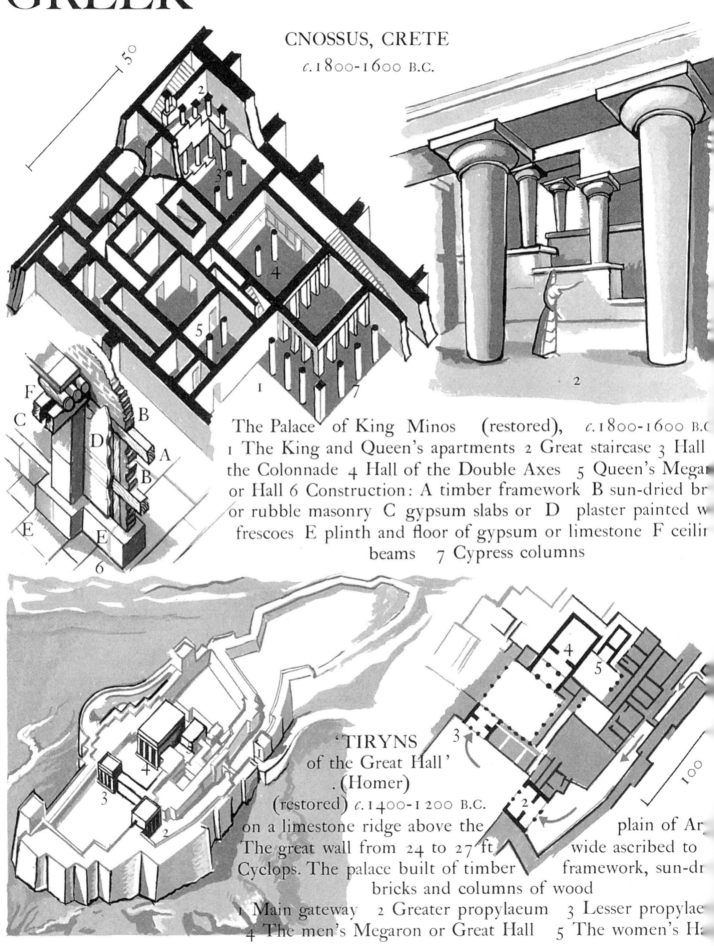

CNOSSUS, CRETE
*c.*1800-1600 B.C.

The Palace of King Minos (restored), *c.*1800-1600 B.C.
1 The King and Queen's apartments 2 Great staircase 3 Hall
the Colonnade 4 Hall of the Double Axes 5 Queen's Mega
or Hall 6 Construction: A timber framework B sun-dried br
or rubble masonry C gypsum slabs or D plaster painted w
frescoes E plinth and floor of gypsum or limestone F ceilin
beams 7 Cypress columns

'TIRYNS
of the Great Hall'
(Homer)
(restored) *c.*1400-1200 B.C.
on a limestone ridge above the plain of Ar
The great wall from 24 to 27 ft. wide ascribed to
Cyclops. The palace built of timber framework, sun-dr
bricks and columns of wood
1 Main gateway 2 Greater propylaeum 3 Lesser propylae
4 The men's Megaron or Great Hall 5 The women's H

THE AEGEAN

The Lion Gate

MYCENAE (restored), *c.*1350 B.C.
The citadel palace of Agamemnon,
Cyclopean walls of boulders weighing 5 to 6
tons were eased into alignment on pebbles

Lion Gate, Mycenae, *c.*1200 B.C.

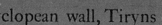

clopean wall, Tiryns   Polygonal, Mycenae   Curvilinear, 7th cent.   Rectangular, 5th cent.

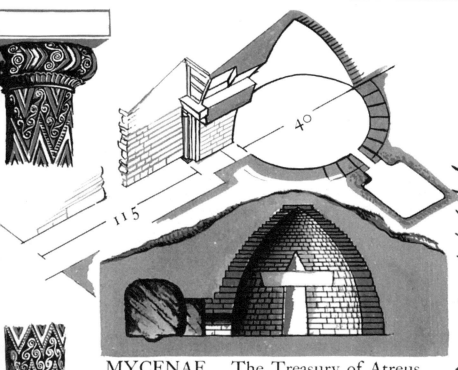

MYCENAE,   The Treasury of Atreus,
1330-1300 B.C.   One of some 40 beehive or
tholos tombs on the Greek mainland. Built of
horizontal overlapping courses of lime-stone or
corbelling without centering. The door-way
flanked by 2 green sandstone half-columns
with a relieving triangle above

GREEK

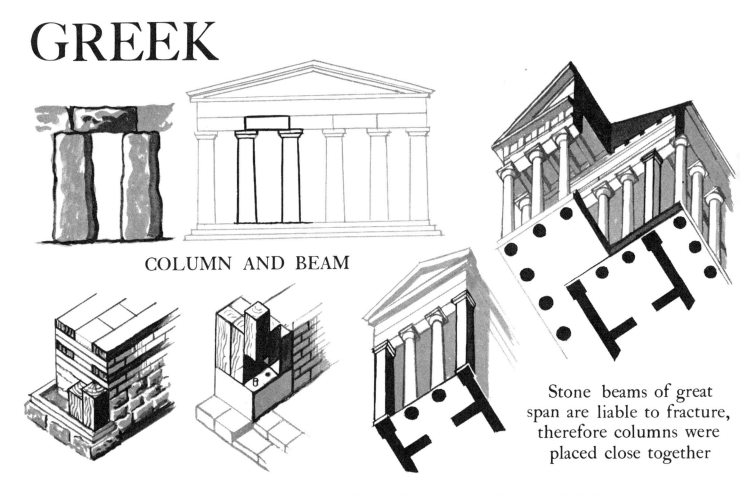

COLUMN AND BEAM

Stone beams of great
span are liable to fracture,
therefore columns were
placed close together

TIMBER TO STONE ANTAE OR PILASTERS

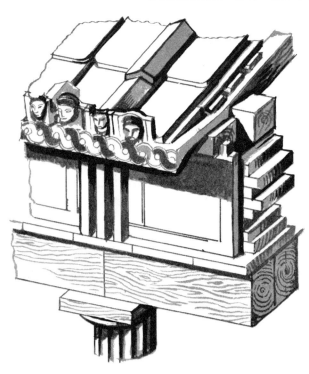

TIMBER construction, *c.*620 B.C.
Doric temple of Apollo, Thermum.
Wooden entablature and columns

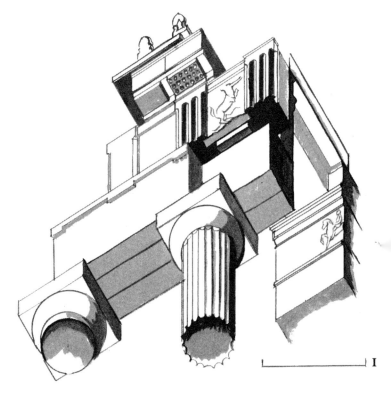

MARBLE construction, *c.*477-438 B.C.
The Parthenon, Athens

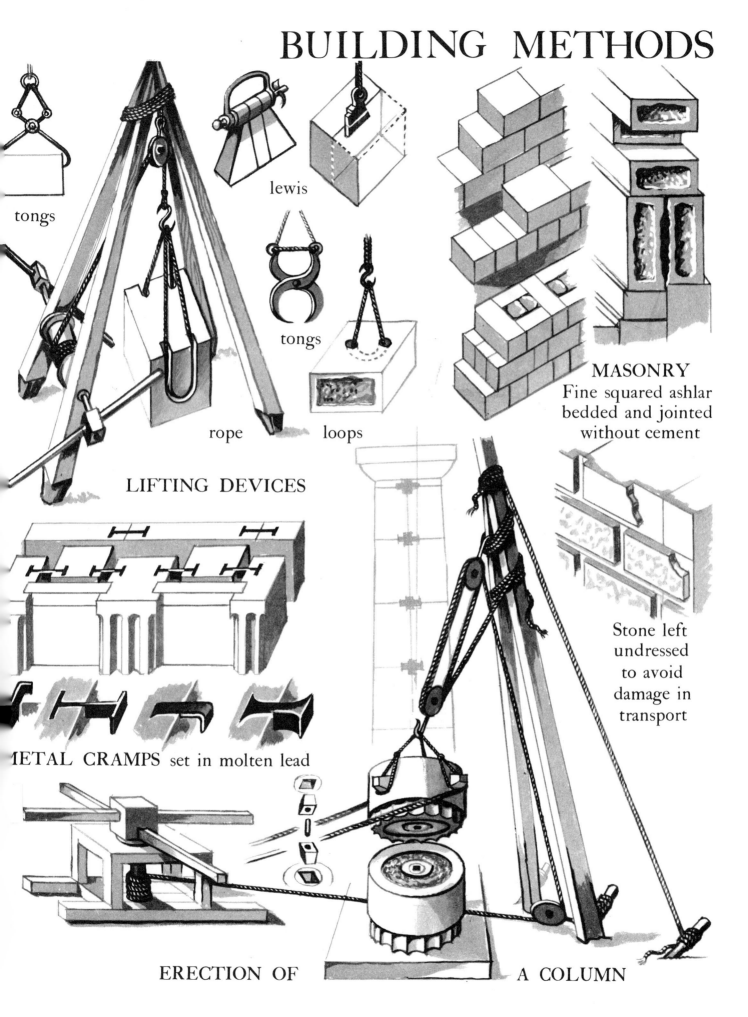

BUILDING METHODS

tongs

lewis

tongs

rope

loops

LIFTING DEVICES

MASONRY
Fine squared ashlar
bedded and jointed
without cement

Stone left
undressed
to avoid
damage in
transport

METAL CRAMPS set in molten lead

ERECTION OF   A COLUMN

GREEK

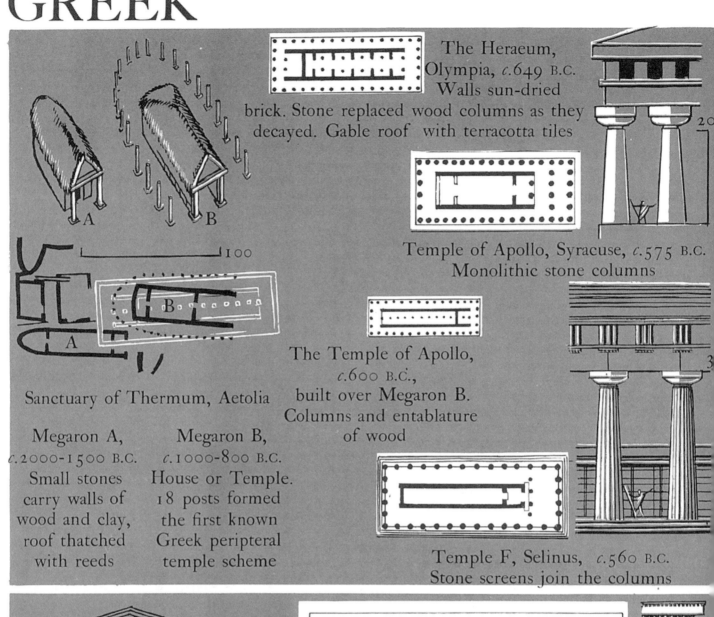

The Heraeum, Olympia, c.649 B.C. Walls sun-dried brick. Stone replaced wood columns as they decayed. Gable roof with terracotta tiles

Temple of Apollo, Syracuse, c.575 B.C. Monolithic stone columns

Sanctuary of Thermum, Aetolia

Megaron A, c.2000-1500 B.C. Small stones carry walls of wood and clay, roof thatched with reeds

Megaron B, c.1000-800 B.C. House or Temple. 18 posts formed the first known Greek peripteral temple scheme

The Temple of Apollo, c.600 B.C., built over Megaron B. Columns and entablature of wood

Temple F, Selinus, c.560 B.C. Stone screens join the columns

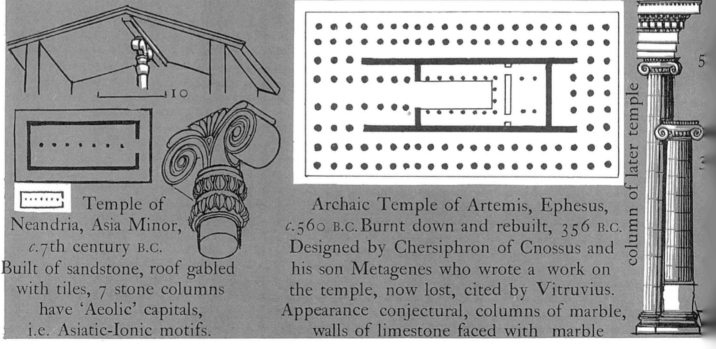

Temple of Neandria, Asia Minor, c.7th century B.C. Built of sandstone, roof gabled with tiles, 7 stone columns have 'Aeolic' capitals, i.e. Asiatic-Ionic motifs.

Archaic Temple of Artemis, Ephesus, c.560 B.C. Burnt down and rebuilt, 356 B.C. Designed by Chersiphron of Cnossus and his son Metagenes who wrote a work on the temple, now lost, cited by Vitruvius. Appearance conjectural, columns of marble, walls of limestone faced with marble

column of later temple

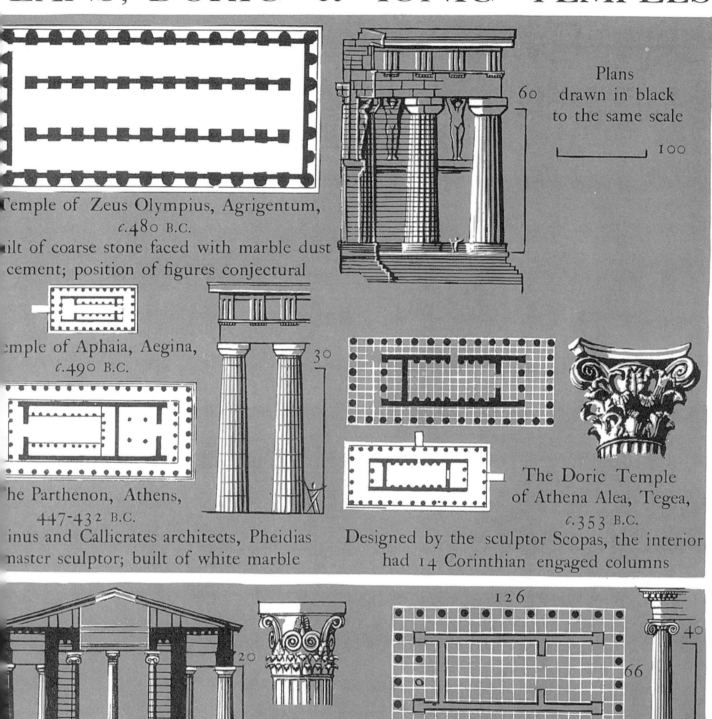

Plans
drawn in black
to the same scale

60

100

Temple of Zeus Olympius, Agrigentum,
c.480 B.C.

Built of coarse stone faced with marble dust
cement; position of figures conjectural

Temple of Aphaia, Aegina,
c.490 B.C.

30

The Parthenon, Athens,
447-432 B.C.

Ictinus and Callicrates architects, Pheidias
master sculptor; built of white marble

The Doric Temple
of Athena Alea, Tegea,
c.353 B.C.

Designed by the sculptor Scopas, the interior
had 14 Corinthian engaged columns

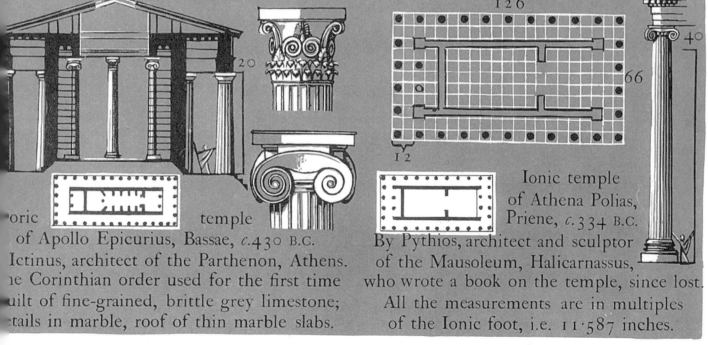

20

126

40

66

12

Doric temple
of Apollo Epicurius, Bassae, c.430 B.C.

Ictinus, architect of the Parthenon, Athens.
The Corinthian order used for the first time
Built of fine-grained, brittle grey limestone;
details in marble, roof of thin marble slabs.

Ionic temple
of Athena Polias,
Priene, c.334 B.C.

By Pythios, architect and sculptor
of the Mausoleum, Halicarnassus,
who wrote a book on the temple, since lost.
All the measurements are in multiples
of the Ionic foot, i.e. 11·587 inches.

GREEK & ROMAN

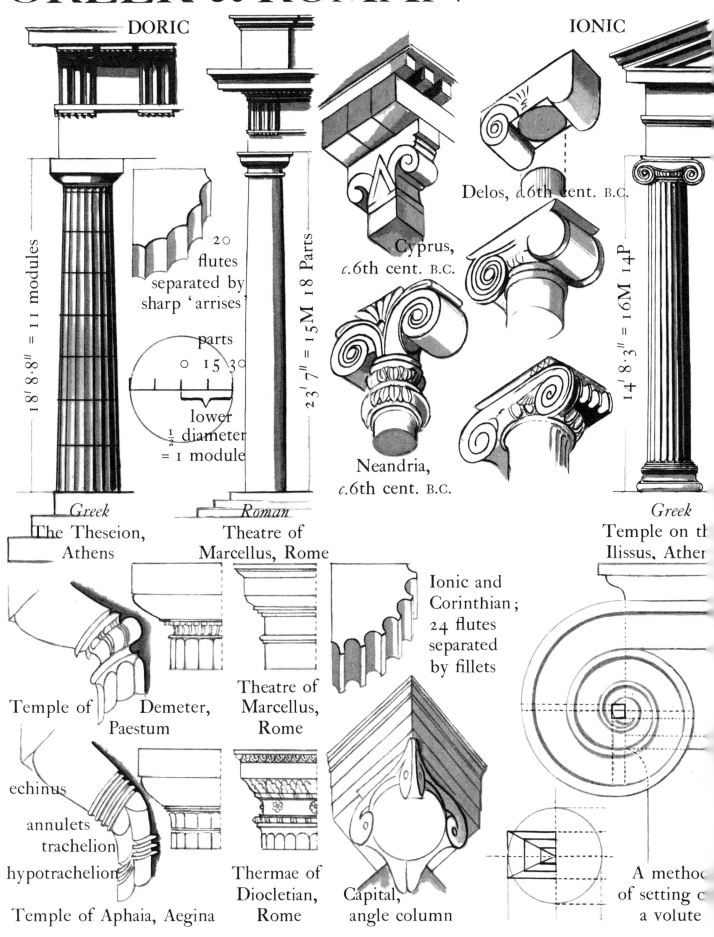

DORIC

IONIC

20 flutes separated by sharp 'arrises'

parts

0 15 3o

lower ½ diameter = 1 module

18' 8.8" = 11 modules

23' 7" = 15M 18 Parts

14' 8.3" = 16M 14P

Delos, *c.*6th cent. B.C.

Cyprus, *c.*6th cent. B.C.

Neandria, *c.*6th cent. B.C.

Greek
The Theseion, Athens

Roman
Theatre of Marcellus, Rome

Greek
Temple on the Ilissus, Athens

echinus

annulets

trachelion

hypotrachelion

Temple of Aphaia, Aegina

Demeter, Paestum

Theatre of Marcellus, Rome

Thermae of Diocletian, Rome

Ionic and Corinthian; 24 flutes separated by fillets

Capital, angle column

A method of setting out a volute

THE FIVE ORDERS

CORINTHIAN

COMPOSITE

TUSCAN

Egypt, Dynasty XIX

Tower of | The Tholos,
the Winds, | Epidaurus,
Athens, *c.*334 | *c.*360 B.C.

$11' 7 \cdot 65'' = 19M \ 28\frac{1}{2}P$

$46' 5'' = 19M \ 2\frac{1}{2}P$

$28' 4'' = 20M$

$16M$

Roman
emple Fortuna
Virilis, Rome

Greek
Choragic
Monument, Athens

Roman
The Pantheon.
Rome

Roman
Arch of
Severus, Rome

Roman
Vitruvius
(IV,7)

issus, Athens

Erechtheum,
Athens

Temple
ortuna Virilis,
Rome

The Olympieum,
Athens, *c.*174 B.C.
Capitals taken
to Rome, 86 B.C.

Temple of
Castor and Pollux,
Rome, A.D. 16

Arch of
Titus,
Rome, A.D. 81

From
*The Five Orders
of Architecture*
by Vignola
(A.D. 1509-73)

GREEK

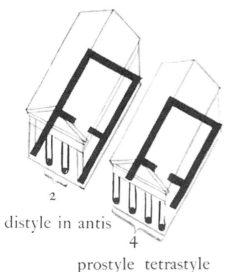

2
distyle in antis

4
prostyle tetrastyle

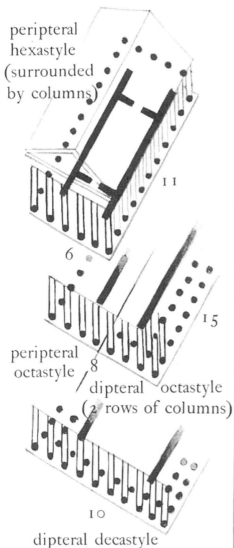

peripteral
hexastyle
(surrounded
by columns)

11

6

15

peripteral
octastyle

8

dipteral octastyle
(2 rows of columns)

10
dipteral decastyle

Classification of columnan
arrangement according to
Vitruvius (III, 2)

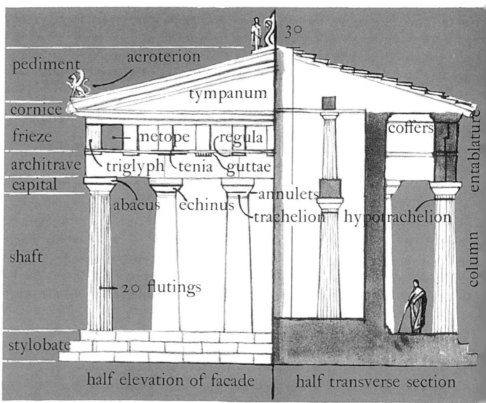

pediment

acroterion

30

tympanum

cornice

frieze

metope regula

coffers

architrave

triglyph tenia guttae

capital

abacus echinus

annulets

shaft

trachelion hypotrachelion

20 flutings

stylobate

half elevation of facade

half transverse section

entablature

column

3

upper
acroterion

4"

8"

antefixa

ridge tiles

40

THE DORIC TEMPLE

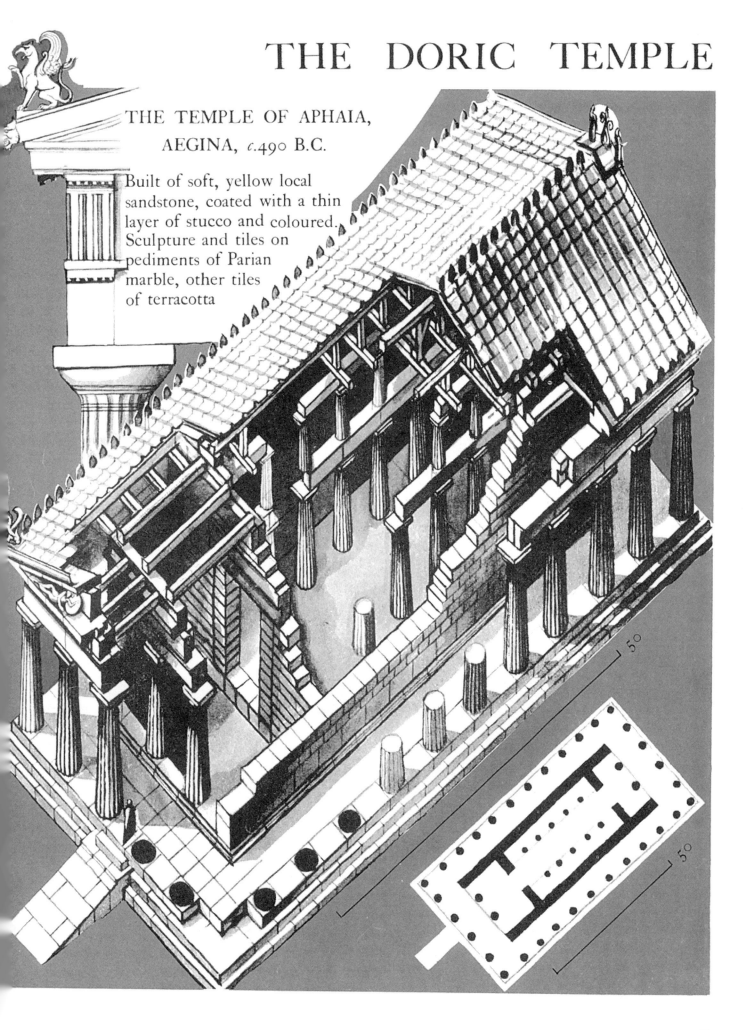

THE TEMPLE OF APHAIA,
AEGINA, c.490 B.C.

Built of soft, yellow local
sandstone, coated with a thin
layer of stucco and coloured.
Sculpture and tiles on
pediments of Parian
marble, other tiles
of terracotta

50

50

GREEK

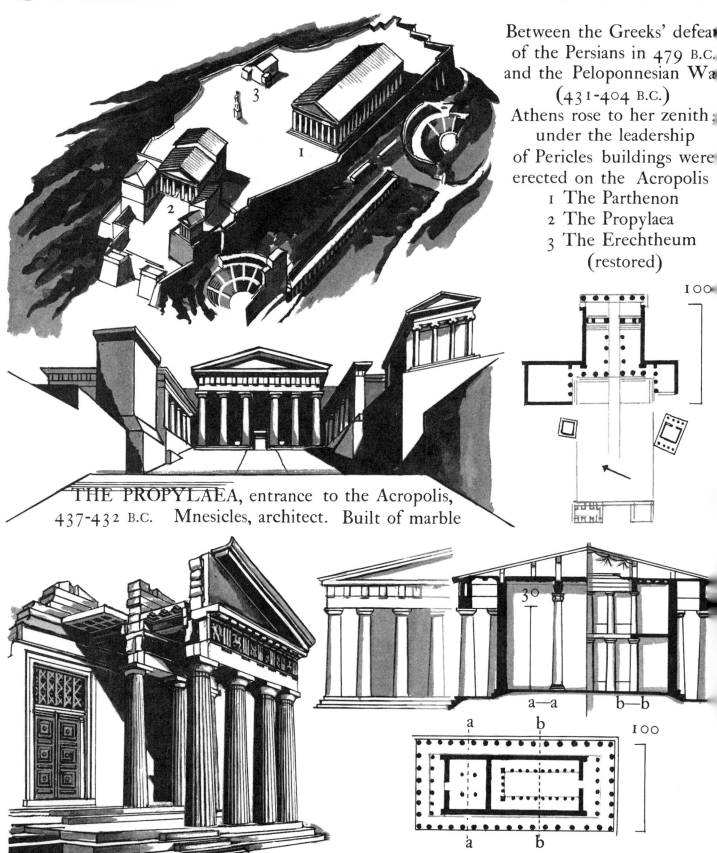

Between the Greeks' defeat
of the Persians in 479 B.C.
and the Peloponnesian War
(431-404 B.C.)
Athens rose to her zenith;
under the leadership
of Pericles buildings were
erected on the Acropolis
 1 The Parthenon
 2 The Propylaea
 3 The Erechtheum
   (restored)

THE PROPYLAEA, entrance to the Acropolis,
437-432 B.C.   Mnesicles, architect. Built of marble

THE PARTHENON, 447-432 B.C. Doric temple
dedicated to Athena.   Ictinus and Callicrates, architect
Phidias, master sculptor. Optical refinements p. 38

THE ERECHTHEUM, 420-406 B.C.
A. Sanctuary of Athena Polias
B. Sanctuaries of Erechtheus and Poseidon

ossible architect Mnesicles.   The caryatids and column capitals may have been designed
y Callimachus, inventor of the Corinthian capital.   Built on 4 levels, irregular in plan
to preserve places sacred to Athens; built of white marble

GREEK

CITY

AEGEAN

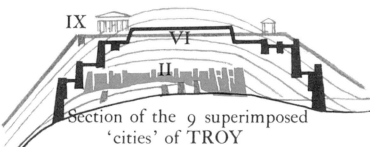

Section of the 9 superimposed
'cities' of TROY
II Prehistoric citadel, c.2600-2300 B.C.
VI Homeric Troy, 1900 B.C.; sacked c.1200 B.C.
IX The Roman acropolis, c.30 B.C.-A.D. 14.

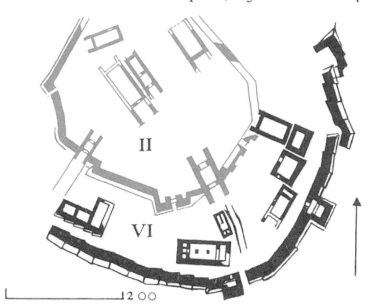

200

Plan of selected buildings, Troy
II Prehistoric citadel VI Homeric Troy

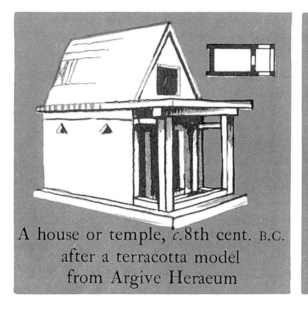

A house or temple, c.8th cent. B.C.
after a terracotta model
from Argive Heraeum

HELLENIC

Little is known of Greek
city planning before
Hippodamus
laid out his native city
MILETUS
c.479 or 466 B.C.

and
'discovered the
method of
dividing up cities'
(Aristotle *Politics*)

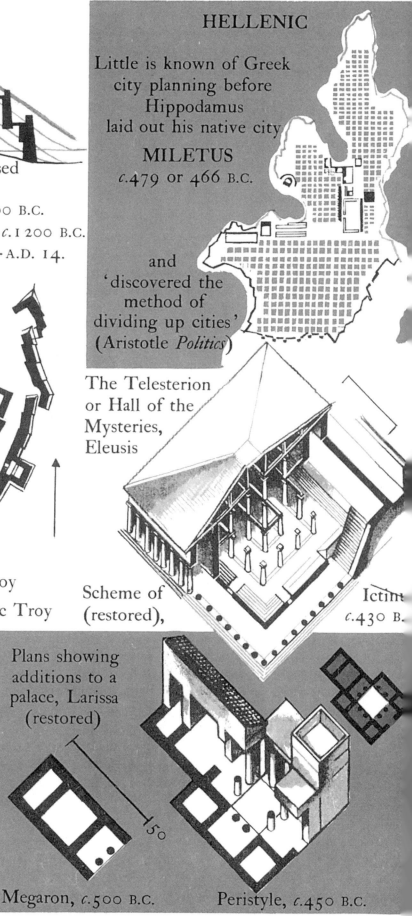

The Telesterion
or Hall of the
Mysteries,
Eleusis

Scheme of   Ictin
(restored),   c.430 B.

Plans showing
additions to a
palace, Larissa
(restored)

50

Megaron, c.500 B.C.   Peristyle, c.450 B.C.

PLANS, BUILDINGS AND HOUSES

HELLENISTIC

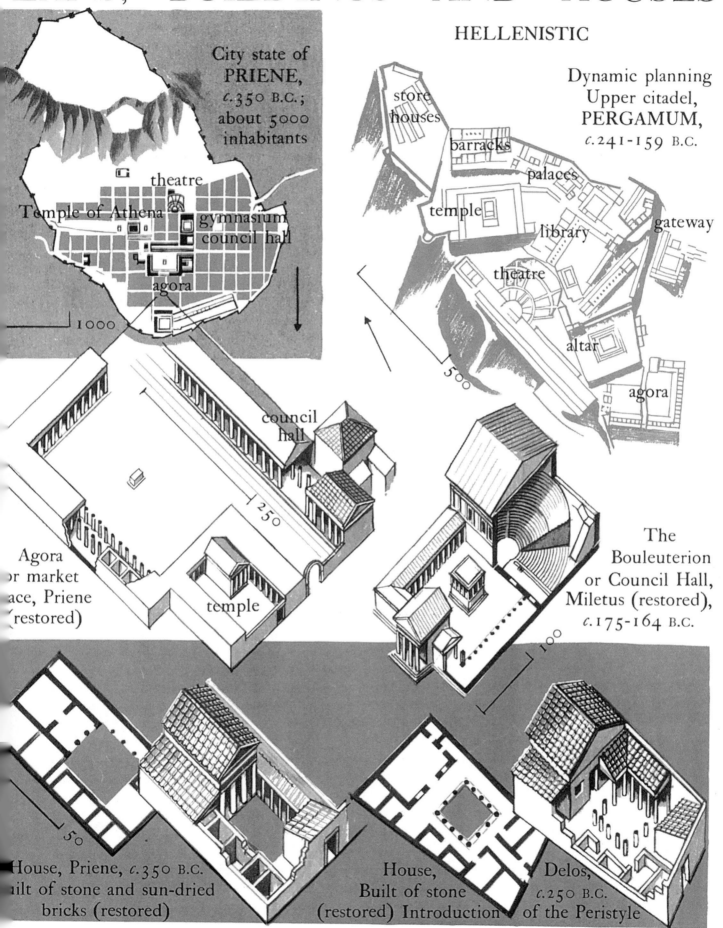

City state of
PRIENE,
*c.*350 B.C.;
about 5000
inhabitants

theatre

Temple of Athena

gymnasium
council hall

agora

1000

Dynamic planning
Upper citadel,
PERGAMUM,
*c.*241-159 B.C.

store
houses

barracks

palaces

temple

library

gateway

theatre

500

altar

agora

council
hall

250

temple

Agora
or market
place, Priene
(restored)

The
Bouleuterion
or Council Hall,
Miletus (restored),
*c.*175-164 B.C.

100

50

House, Priene, *c.*350 B.C.
built of stone and sun-dried
bricks (restored)

House,
Built of stone
(restored) Introduction

Delos,
*c.*250 B.C.
of the Peristyle

GREEK REFINEMENTS

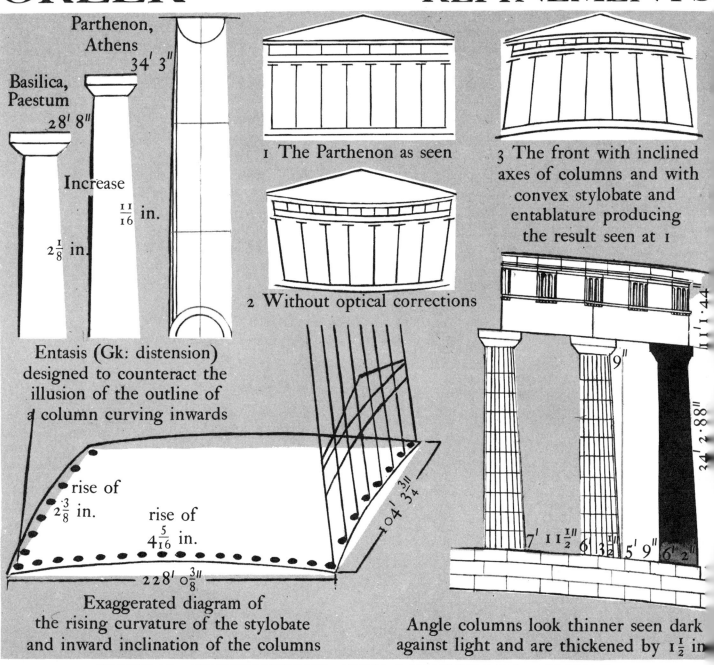

Parthenon,
Athens
34' 3"

Basilica,
Paestum
28' 8"

Increase
$\frac{11}{16}$ in.

$2\frac{1}{8}$ in.

1 The Parthenon as seen

2 Without optical corrections

3 The front with inclined
axes of columns and with
convex stylobate and
entablature producing
the result seen at 1

Entasis (Gk: distension)
designed to counteract the
illusion of the outline of
a column curving inwards

rise of
$2\frac{3}{8}$ in.

rise of
$4\frac{5}{16}$ in.

104' 3¾"

228' 0⅜"

Exaggerated diagram of
the rising curvature of the stylobate
and inward inclination of the columns

11'1·44"

9"

24'2·88"

7' 11½" 6' 3½" 5' 9" 6' 2"

Angle columns look thinner seen dark
against light and are thickened by $1\frac{1}{2}$ in

OPTICAL CORRECTIONS, THE PARTHENON, ATHENS

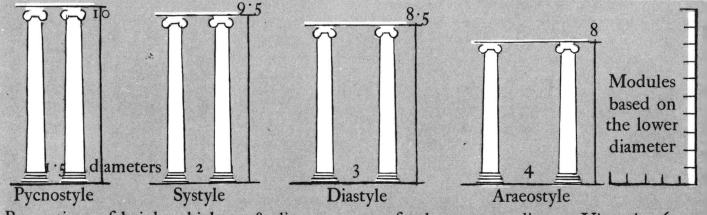

10

9·5

8·5

8

Modules
based on
the lower
diameter

1·5 diameters   2   3   4

Pycnostyle   Systyle   Diastyle   Araeostyle

Proportions of height, thickness & distance apart of columns according to Vitruvius (III,3

The Tholos,
Epidaurus, c. 360 B.C.
by the sculptor-architect
Polycleitus the Younger;
built of sandstone and marble

The Choragic
Monument of Lysicrates,
Athens, c. 334 B.C.
Podium of limestone,
upper part white marble,
Corinthian order used
externally for the first time

The Tower of the Winds, Athens,
c. 50 B.C.   Clock-tower built of marble

ROMAN

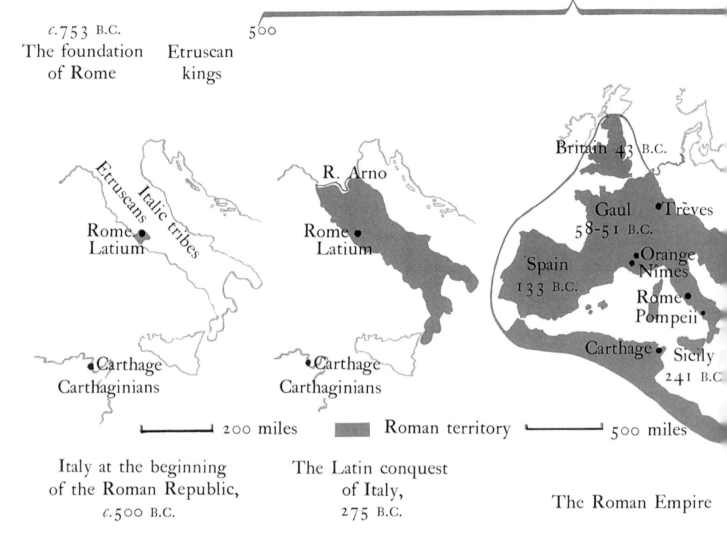

c.753 B.C.
The foundation of Rome

Etruscan kings

500

Italy at the beginning of the Roman Republic, c.500 B.C.

The Latin conquest of Italy, 275 B.C.

200 miles   Roman territory   500 miles

The Roman Empire

Early Rome, with its Republican magistrates, town-council (senatus) and town-meetings (comitia), by a series of systematic conquests created an Empire round the Mediterranean consisting of different nationalities accepted as allies. The Roman Empire became a fusion of the practical Western idea of one universal society in which all men might live in conformity with Roman law and the Oriental conception of an Emperor-God with a throne-altar demanding a common worship and loyalty. This union between the West and the East was a continual source of weakness and led to the ultimate division of the Empire. The Romans built roads and bridges for swift communication, military camps with a simple set plan (later incorporated in many city-plans) for speed of construction, and government and civic buildings, which were both useful and symbolic of Roman law and order.

Greek Hellenic Period   Hellenistic

775/6

429/8 — Plato — 347
384 Aristotle 322
342-Epicurus-270
326?-Zeno-264? (Stoicism)

323

INTRODUCTION

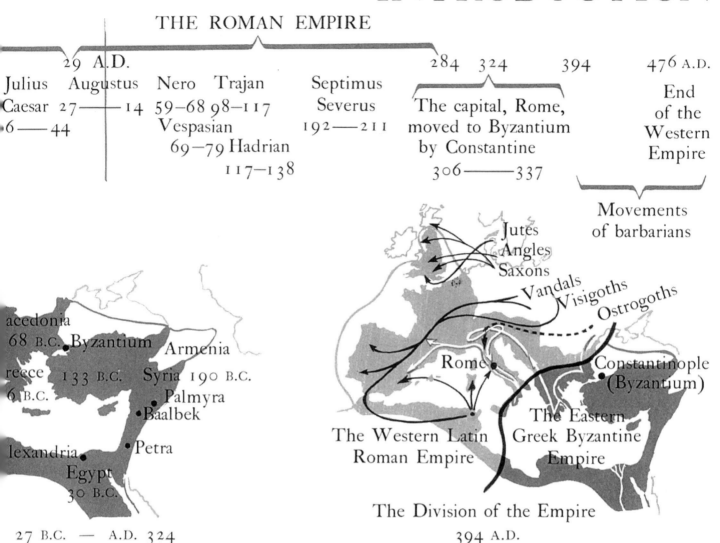

THE ROMAN EMPIRE

29 A.D.					284 324	394	476 A.D.

Julius Augustus Nero Trajan Septimus
Caesar 27——|—14 59–68 98–117 Severus
6——44 Vespasian 192——211
69–79 Hadrian
117–138

The capital, Rome,
moved to Byzantium
by Constantine
306——337

End
of the
Western
Empire

Movements
of barbarians

27 B.C. — A.D. 324

The Division of the Empire
394 A.D.

ring the Republic kiln-baked bricks and
one blocks with or without mortar were
d in building. The invention of concrete
olutionised construction in the Empire.
ncrete was used with a facing for protec-
n and a surface finish, & there is a sharp
tinction between the art of the engineer
nstructing arches, vaults and domes and
applied art of decoration with columns
and pilasters, marbles and mosaics.

The Romans invented all possible variations
in the plans of buildings which were copied
by later architects. *The Ten Books on
Architecture* by Marcus Vitruvius Pollio, a
Roman architect and engineer who lived in
the 1st century B.C. was widely read in
the Renaissance and later.

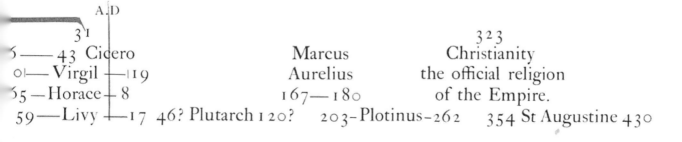

A.D
31
5——43 Cicero
o|—Virgil—|19
55—Horace—|8
59—Livy—|17 46? Plutarch 120?

Marcus
Aurelius
167—180
203-Plotinus-262

323
Christianity
the official religion
of the Empire.
354 St Augustine 430

ROMAN

The Forum Romanum (restored),
looking towards the Tabularium

Forum and basilica,
Silchester, England,
c.A.D. 50-100

THE
FORUMS,
ROME (restored)

I Forum Romanum, from
c.5th century B.C. II Julium, 49 B.C.-A.D.14.
III Augustus, 28 B.C.-A.D. 14. IV Vespasian,   A.D. 67-79.
V Nerva, c.A.D. 97. VI Trajan, A.D. 100-117.
TEMPLES: 1 Saturn, 44 B.C. 2 Concord, 7 B.C. 3 Venus Genetrix, 49 B.C.
4 Mars Ultor, 14-2 B.C. 5 Minerva, 28 B.C.-A.D. 14. 6 Divus Julius, 8 B.C.-A.D. 14.
7 Castor and Pollux, A.D. 6. 8 Peace, A.D. 67-79. 9 Vespasian, A.D. 94. 10 Trajan, A.D. 100-11
11 Venus and Rome, A.D. 123-135. 12 Faustina, A.D. 141. 13 Vesta, A.D. 205.
BASILICAS: 14 Aemilia, c.179 B.C. 15 Julia, 46 B.C. 16 Trajan, A.D. 100-117.
17 Constantine, A.D. 310-313.
BUILDINGS: 18 Tabularium, 78 B.C. 19 Curia (Senate House), 49 B.C.-A.D.14. 20 House
the Vestal Virgins, c.A.D.17. 21 Colosseum, A.D. 70-82. 22 Arch of Septimus Severus, A.D. 2(

BUILDINGS AND PLANS, ROME

Drawn to the same scale |⸻⸻⸻⸻| 500

The Thermae of Caracalla,
Rome, *c.* A.D. 212-217

Stands on a platform 20 ft high
containing store-rooms, furnaces,
hypocausts and hot-air ducts;
room for more than 1600 bathers

1 Main entrance
2 Apodyteria—undressing rooms
3 Tepidarium—tepid bath
4 Calidarium—hot-air bath
5 Warm baths
6 Hot baths
7 Frigidarium—
   open-air cold bath
8 Palaestra, peristyles
9 Lecture halls and
   libraries

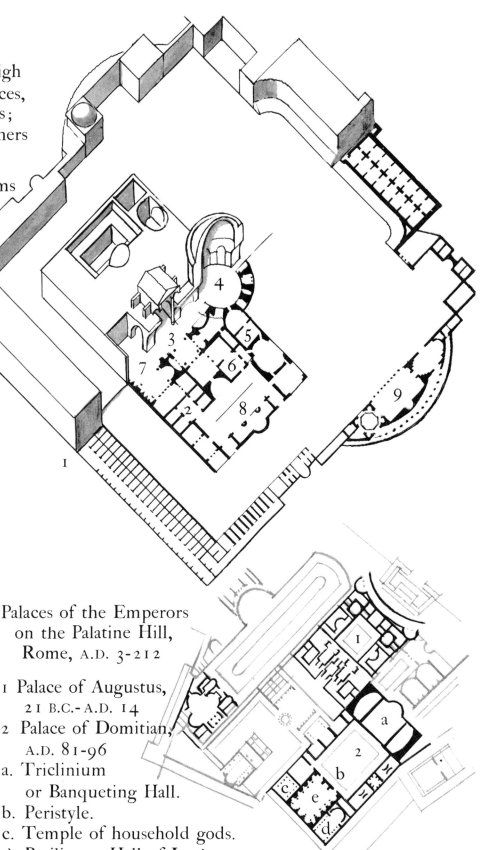

The Pantheon, Rome,
A.D. 120-124

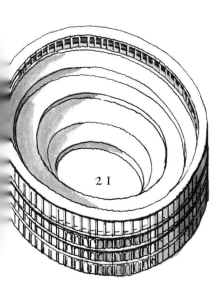

Palaces of the Emperors
on the Palatine Hill,
Rome, A.D. 3-212

1 Palace of Augustus,
   21 B.C.-A.D. 14
2 Palace of Domitian,
   A.D. 81-96
a. Triclinium
   or Banqueting Hall.
b. Peristyle.
c. Temple of household gods.
d. Basilica or Hall of Justice.
e. Tablinum or Throne Room

ROMAN

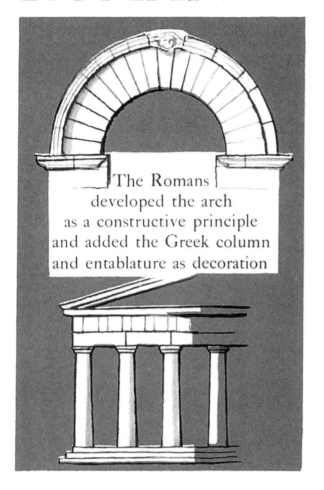

The Romans developed the arch as a constructive principle and added the Greek column and entablature as decoration

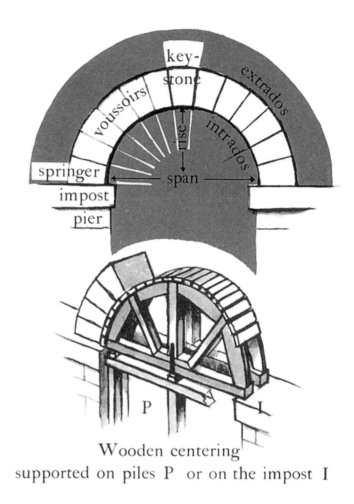

key-stone

extrados

voussoirs

intrados

rise

springer

span

impost

pier

Wooden centering
supported on piles P or on the impost I

Ribs of baked brick set on wooden centering to receive concrete

Methods of constructing stone and concrete vaults

THE ARCH

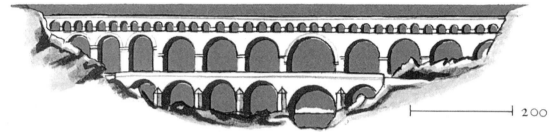

Arches supported on piers: Aqueduct, Pont du Gard, Nîmes, *c.*A.D. 150

Theatre of Marcellus, Rome, 23–13 B.C.

Theatre, Arles, 1st-3rd cent. A.D.

Construction of arches on piers with non-constructional facing of columns and entablature

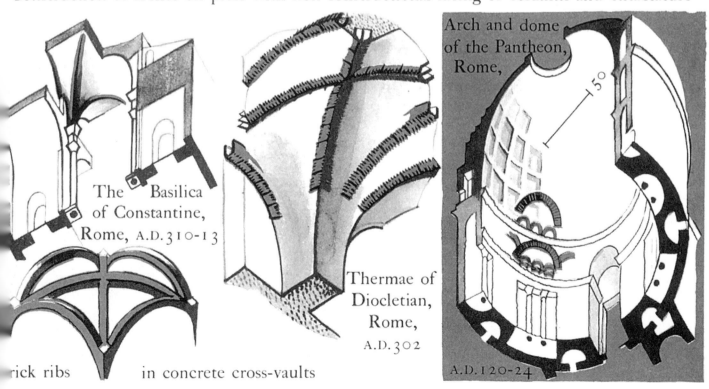

The Basilica of Constantine, Rome, A.D. 310–13

Thermae of Diocletian, Rome, A.D. 302

Arch and dome of the Pantheon, Rome, A.D. 120–24

rick ribs   in concrete cross-vaults

ROMAN

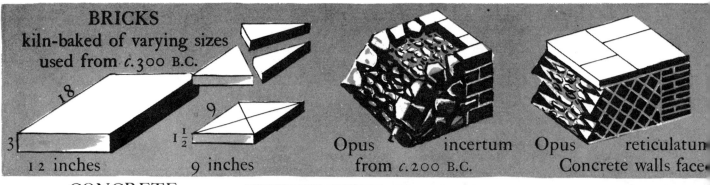

BRICKS
kiln-baked of varying sizes
used from *c.*300 B.C.

18
3
12 inches

9
1½
9 inches

Opus   incertum
from *c.*200 B.C.

Opus   reticulatum
Concrete walls face

CONCRETE
used by the Romans from the
2nd century B.C., consisting of
sand, gravel, pebbles, chippings
of stone, mixed with a cement
of lime and water and spread
over a temporary wooden or
permanent brick centering, to
solidify into the required shape
–arch, vault or dome. The dead
weight rested upon supporting
walls or piers without exerting
an outward thrust. Pozzolana,
a volcanic rock found near
Rome, made a concrete of great
hardness and durability.
Concrete surfaces were faced
with stucco, brick or marble
for protection and finish.

MASONRY

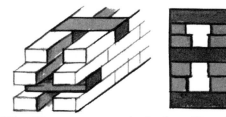

The Romans copied the Greek
technique, building courses of
dressed blocks, held by through
stones laid dry without mortar
or with iron cramps and dowels
set in molten lead. The space
between the courses was left
empty or filled with undressed
stones, earth or concrete.

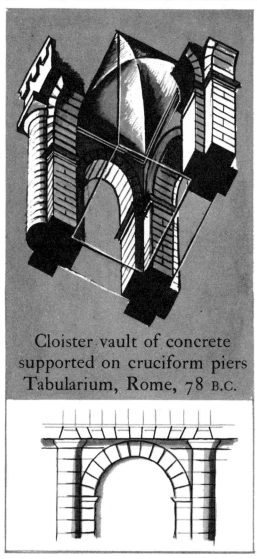

Cloister vault of concrete
supported on cruciform piers
Tabularium, Rome, 78 B.C.

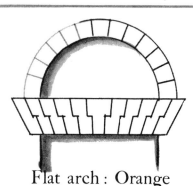

Flat arch : Orange

Concrete barrel vault
The Colosseum, Rome.
A.D. 70-82

MATERIALS & METHODS

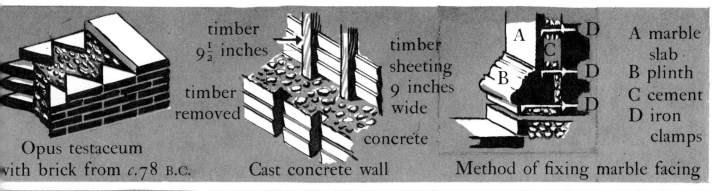

timber
9½ inches

timber
removed

timber
sheeting
9 inches
wide

concrete

A marble
slab
B plinth
C cement
D iron
clamps

Opus testaceum
with brick from c.78 B.C.

Cast concrete wall

Method of fixing marble facing

Cross-vault
built of brick ribs
and filled in with concrete
Villa Sette Bassi, near
Rome, c.A.D. 123-134

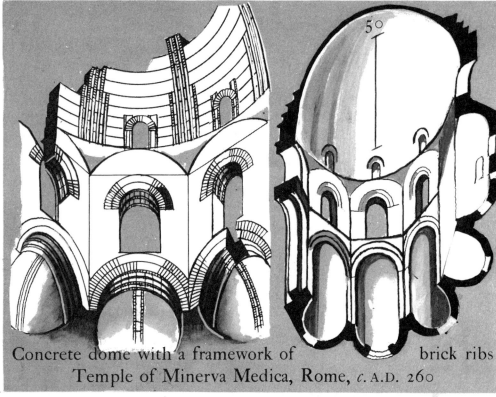

Concrete dome with a framework of
Temple of Minerva Medica, Rome, c.A.D. 260

brick ribs

The
Pretorium,
Musmiyeh,
c.A.D. 180

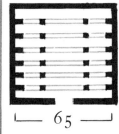

The Basilica,
Shakka,
c.A.D. 175-200

Syria:
buildings of dressed stone
continued in the period of
Early Christian architecture in
the 5th to 7th centuries

ROMAN

Construction of dome

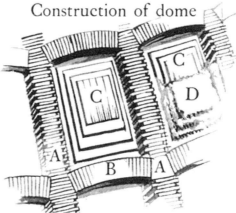

A Brick ribs   B Brick Arches
C Wooden moulds D Concrete

Concealed brick arches
link together 8 massive
brick piers supporting
the dome

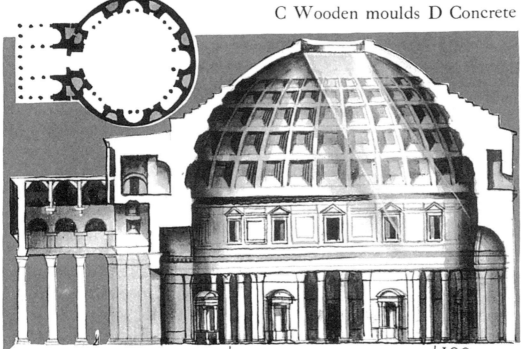

The Pantheon, Rome, A.D. 120-24. Erected by Hadrian

The Temple of Vesta, Tivoli (restored), 27 B.C.-A.D.
Foundations: tufa.   Podium and walls: concrete.
Columns and door: travertine. Roof: probably a low
concrete dome

The Colosseum, Rome, A.D. 70-82
Designed for about 45,000 spectators. 80 piers support 3 tiers of arcading. Decorative use of superimposed orders of ¾ external Doric, Ionic and Corinthian columns. Foundations: lava. Walls: brick and tufa. Vaults: pumice-stone. Facade: travertine blocks held by metal cramps. Columns and seats: marble

3rd storey Corinthian

2nd storey Ionic

Top storey Corinthian

Ground storey Doric

200

The Temple of Venus, Baalbek (restored), c. A.D. 245

ROMAN

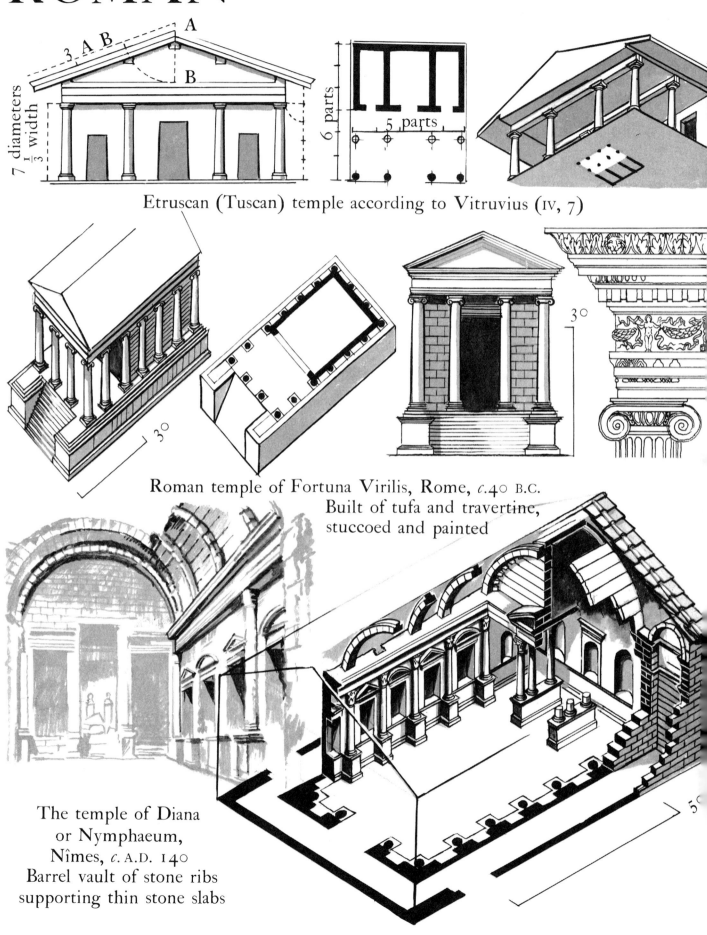

7 diameters
⅓ width

3 A B

A

B

6 parts

5 parts

Etruscan (Tuscan) temple according to Vitruvius (IV, 7)

30

30

30

Roman temple of Fortuna Virilis, Rome, c.40 B.C.
Built of tufa and travertine,
stuccoed and painted

The temple of Diana
or Nymphaeum,
Nîmes, c. A.D. 140
Barrel vault of stone ribs
supporting thin stone slabs

5

TEMPLES

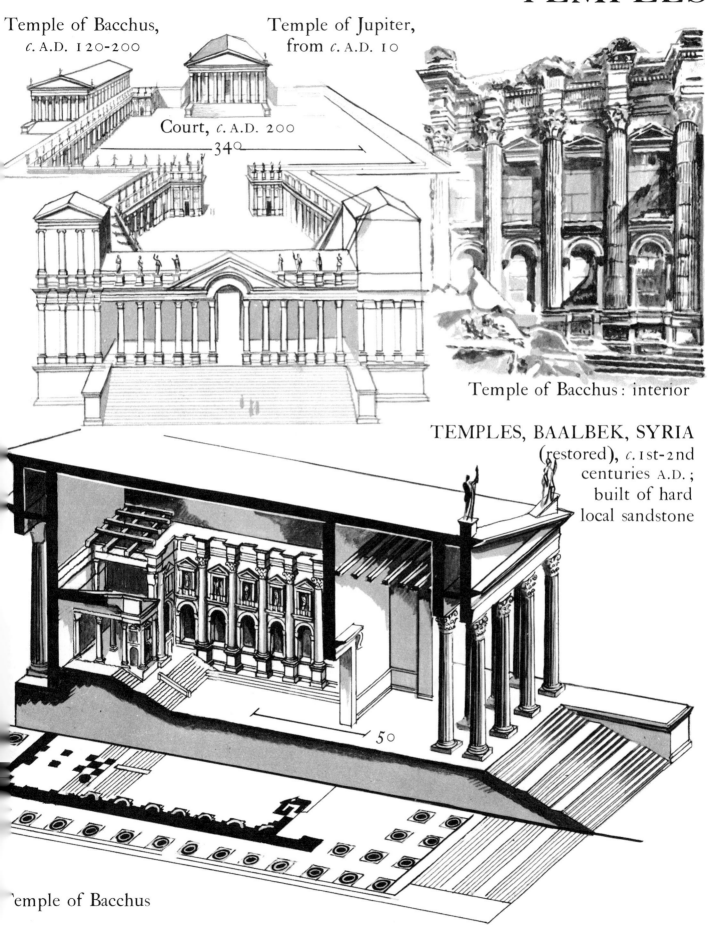

Temple of Bacchus,
c. A.D. 120-200

Temple of Jupiter,
from *c.* A.D. 10

Court, *c.* A.D. 200

340

Temple of Bacchus: interior

TEMPLES, BAALBEK, SYRIA
(restored), *c.* 1st-2nd
centuries A.D.;
built of hard
local sandstone

50

Temple of Bacchus

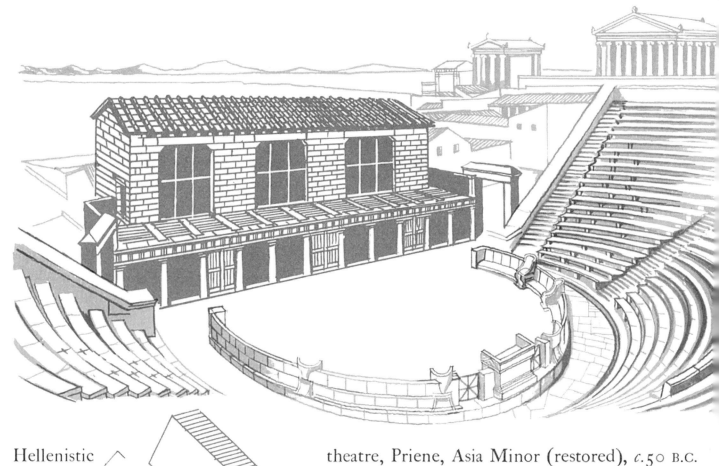

Hellenistic theatre, Priene, Asia Minor (restored), *c.*50 B.C.

Plan of a Greek theatre based on 3 squares within the orchestra circle (Vitruvius, v.7)

The early Greek theatre consisted of an auditorium (simply a hill slope with stone seats), a semi-circular orchestra where the chorus sang and danced, and a wooden stage from which a single actor would hold a dialogue with the chorus. The number of actors was raised to two or three by Aeschylus (525-456 B.C.) and Sophocles (495-406 B.C.), who also introduced painted scenery and a dressing hut or skene. In the 4th century B.C. a wooden skene A was erected with a proscenium B having a row of columns, usually Doric, 8-12 ft from the skene wall supporting a stage of planks called the logeion or speaking-place C. Three doors in the skene wall were for entrances and exits of actors. At the two ends of the proscenium were the parodoi or open passage-ways D.

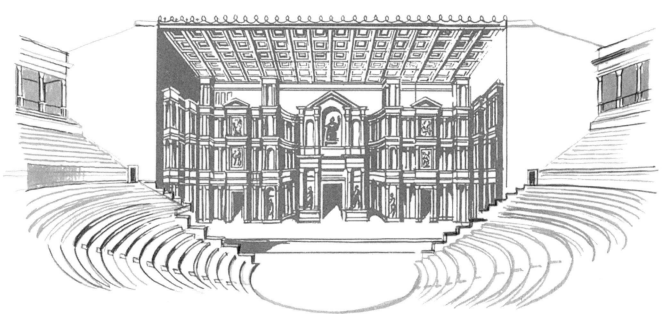

e Theatre, Orange (restored), *c.*A.D.50. Designed to seat 7000. Stage 5 ft high, 23 ft deep.
Built up on stone and concrete piers.
A Semi-circular cavea or auditorium
Proscenium replaced by a frons scaenae
Covered   passages—vomitoria
roduction   of a stage curtain

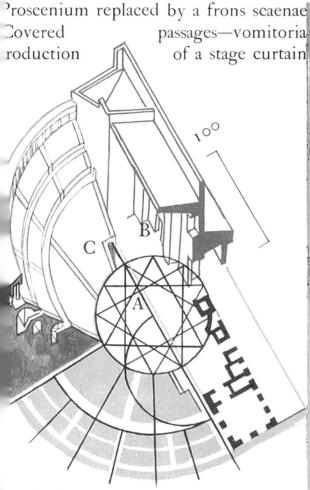

 of a Roman theatre based on 4 equi-
al triangles in a circle (Vitruvius V,6)

A Renaissance adaptation of a Roman theatre. The Teatro Olympico, Vicenza, Italy, designed by Palladio and completed by Scamozzi, A.D. 1584

ROMAN

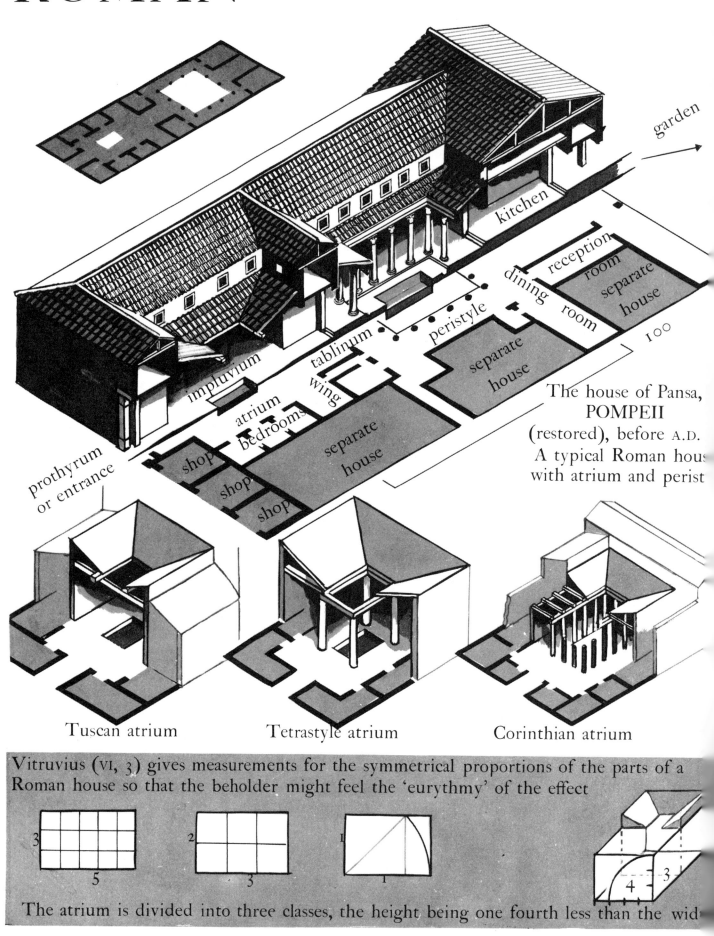

garden

kitchen

reception room

dining room

separate house

peristyle

tablinum

wing

separate house

atrium

impluvium

bedrooms

separate house

shop

shop

shop

prothyrum or entrance

100

The house of Pansa, POMPEII (restored), before A.D.
A typical Roman hous with atrium and perist

Tuscan atrium

Tetrastyle atrium

Corinthian atrium

Vitruvius (VI, 3) gives measurements for the symmetrical proportions of the parts of a Roman house so that the beholder might feel the 'eurythmy' of the effect

3   5

2   3

1   1

4   3

The atrium is divided into three classes, the height being one fourth less than the wid

THE ROMAN HOUSE

Insula or Block of Flats, OSTIA, near Rome (restored)
In Ostia and Rome 4- or 5-storey flats were limited to 65 feet in height by Augustus
30 B.C.-A.D. 14) and to 58 feet by Trajan (A.D. 98-117). They were mostly brick-faced,
occasionally stuccoed, the windows glazed with mica or glass.

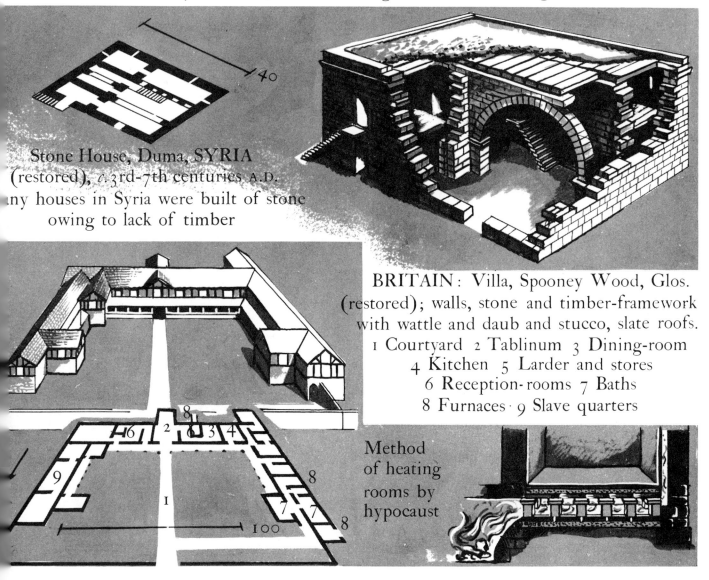

Stone House, Duma, SYRIA
(restored), c. 3rd-7th centuries A.D.
ny houses in Syria were built of stone
owing to lack of timber

BRITAIN: Villa, Spooney Wood, Glos.
(restored); walls, stone and timber-framework
with wattle and daub and stucco, slate roofs.
1 Courtyard 2 Tablinum 3 Dining-room
4 Kitchen 5 Larder and stores
6 Reception-rooms 7 Baths
8 Furnaces · 9 Slave quarters

Method
of heating
rooms by
hypocaust

ROMAN

THERMA[

The Tepidarium: the concrete vault rested on eight piers of masonry with granite colu[

64

PALACE

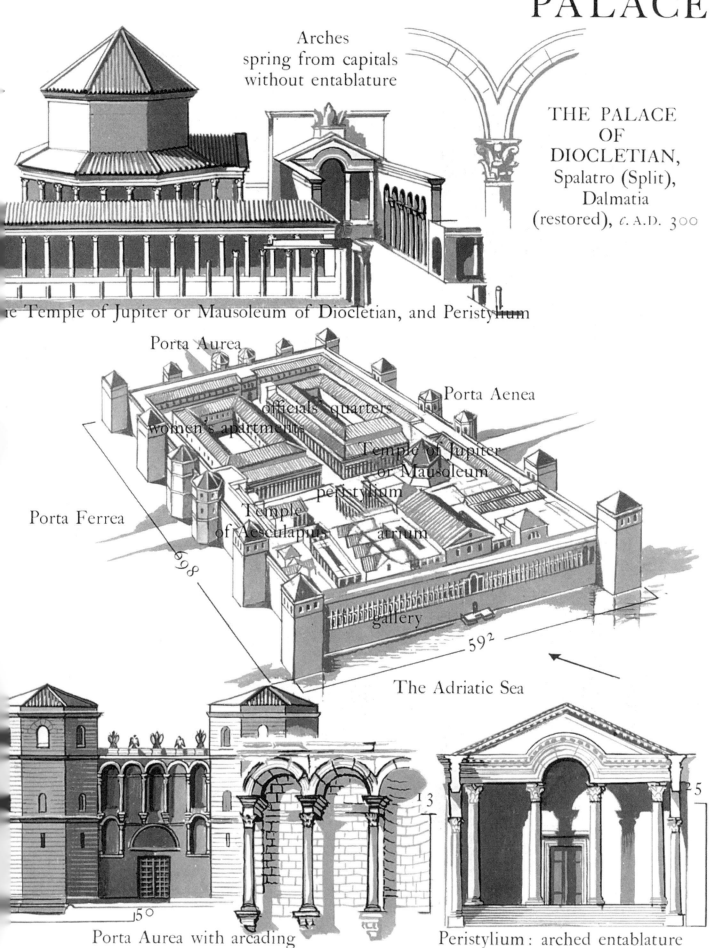

Arches
spring from capitals
without entablature

THE PALACE
OF
DIOCLETIAN,
Spalatro (Split),
Dalmatia
(restored), *c.* A.D. 300

The Temple of Jupiter or Mausoleum of Diocletian, and Peristylium

Porta Aurea

Porta Aenea

officials' quarters

women's apartments

Temple of Jupiter
or Mausoleum

peristylium

Porta Ferrea

Temple
of Aesculapius

atrium

698

gallery

59²

The Adriatic Sea

Porta Aurea with arcading

13

5º

Peristylium: arched entablature

25

65

ROMAN

Triumphal Arches with one opening

Arch of Augustus, Susa,
Piedmont, *c.* A.D. 8

Arch of Titus, Rome, A.D. 70
Earliest use of the Composite order.

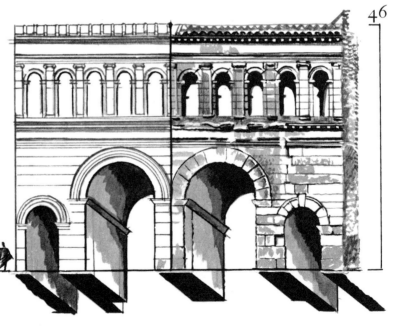

Tomb of the Julii,
Provence, S. Remy,
c. 30 B.C.–A.D. 14

Town gateway with four archways
The Porte S. André, Augustodonum (Autun).
An arcaded gallery with Ionic pilasters creates
an antiphonal response with the rise and fall
of the large and small arches below

Trajan's
Column,
Rome,
A.D. 114.

ARCHES AND MONUMENTS

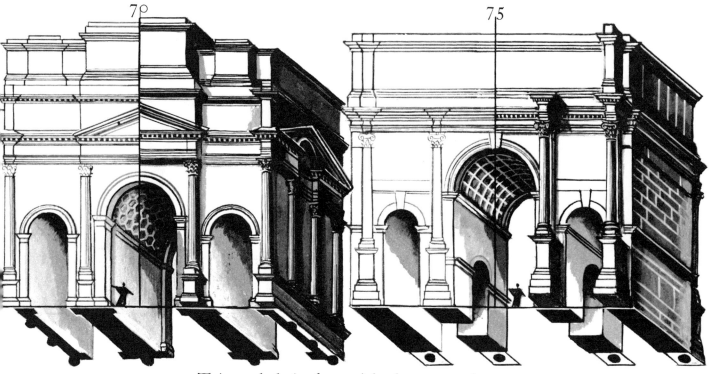

70   75

Triumphal Arches with three openings.

Arch of Tiberius, Orange, *c.* A.D. 2 1   Arch of Septimus Severus, Rome, A.D. 2OO

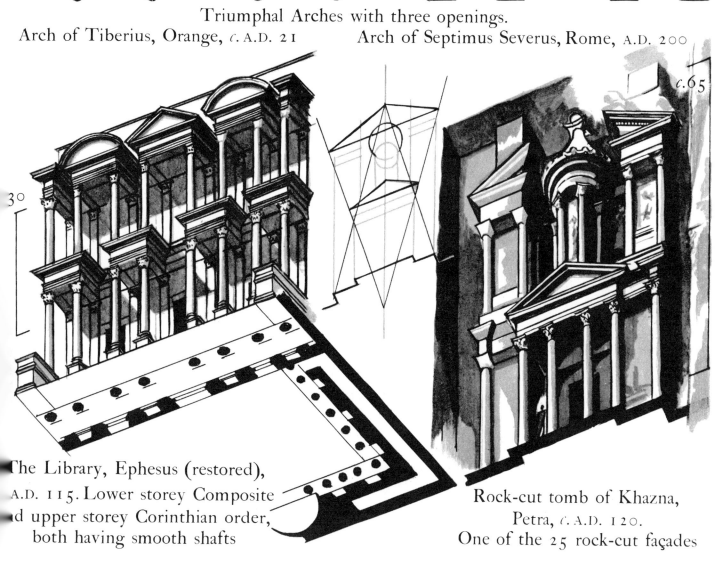

30   *c.*65

The Library, Ephesus (restored),
A.D. 115. Lower storey Composite
and upper storey Corinthian order,
both having smooth shafts

Rock-cut tomb of Khazna,
Petra, *c.* A.D. 12O.
One of the 25 rock-cut façades

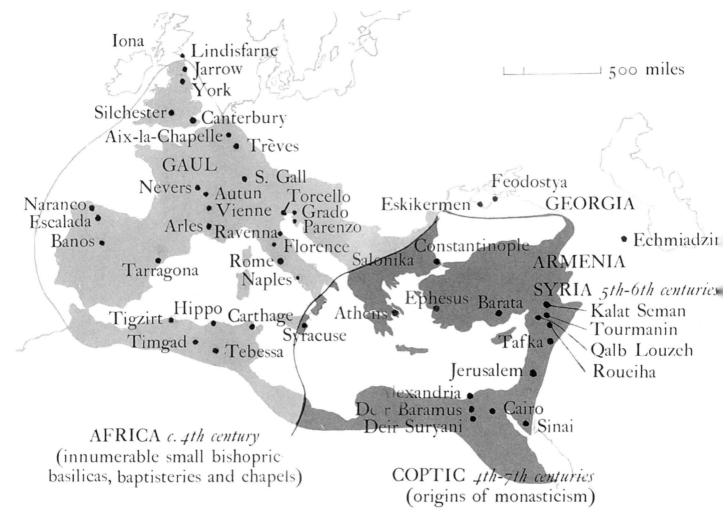

Iona
Lindisfarne
Jarrow
York
Silchester
Canterbury
Aix-la-Chapelle
Trèves
GAUL
S. Gall
Nevers
Autun
Torcello
Eskikermen
Feodostya
GEORGIA
Naranco
Vienne
Grado
Echmiadzir
Escalada
Arles
Ravenna
Parenzo
Constantinople
ARMENIA
Banos
Florence
Salonika
SYRIA 5th-6th centuries
Rome
Naples
Ephesus
Barata
Kalat Seman
Tarragona
Athens
Tourmanin
Tigzirt
Hippo
Carthage
Tafka
Qalb Louzeh
Timgad
Tebessa
Syracuse
Roueiha
Jerusalem
Alexandria
Deir Baramus
Cairo
Deir Suryani
Sinai

500 miles

AFRICA *c. 4th century*
(innumerable small bishopric
basilicas, baptisteries and chapels)

COPTIC *4th-7th centuries*
(origins of monasticism)

Christianity accepted as the state religion in A.D. 337. Basilican churches were built throughout the Roman Empire to house large congregations. In contrast to Classical temples little regard was given to their external appearanc The term 'basilica' was used f churches from the 4th centur plans being similar to those o Roman basilicas or Halls of Justice.

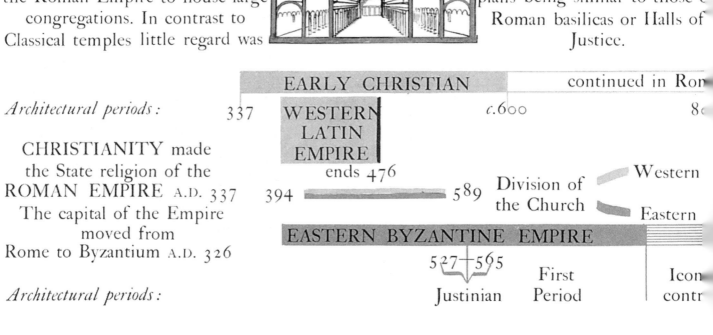

	EARLY CHRISTIAN		continued in Ror
Architectural periods: 337	WESTERN LATIN EMPIRE	*c.600*	8

ends 476

CHRISTIANITY made the State religion of the ROMAN EMPIRE A.D. 337 The capital of the Empire moved from Rome to Byzantium A.D. 326

394 — 589   Division of the Church

Western

Eastern

EASTERN BYZANTINE EMPIRE

527 — 595   First Period   Icon contr

Justinian

Architectural periods:

BYZANTINE INTRODUCTION

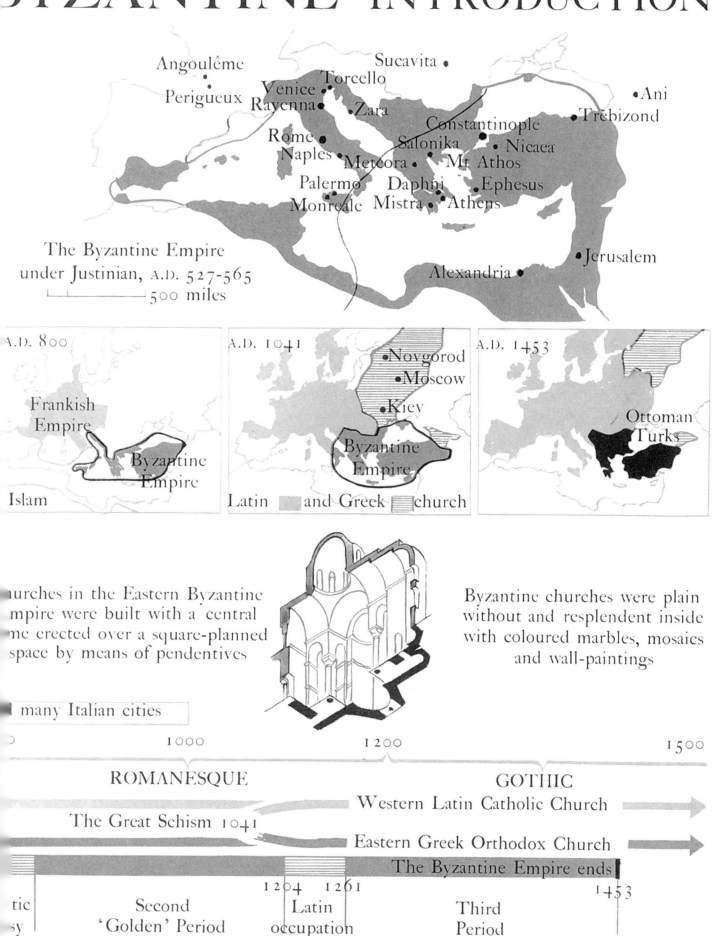

Angoulême •

Sucavita •

Torcello •

Venice •

Rayenna • Zara •

Rome • Constantinople •

Naples • Salonika • Nicaea •

Meteora • Mt Athos •

Palermo • Daphni • Ephesus •

Monreale • Mistra • Athens •

Alexandria •

Jerusalem •

• Ani

Trebizond •

Perigueux •

The Byzantine Empire
under Justinian, A.D. 527-565

├────────────┤ 500 miles

A.D. 800

Frankish
Empire

Byzantine
Empire

Islam

A.D. 1041

• Novgorod
• Moscow
• Kiev

Byzantine
Empire

Latin [ ] and Greek [ ] church

A.D. 1453

Ottoman
Turks

...urches in the Eastern Byzantine
...pire were built with a central
...me erected over a square-planned
...space by means of pendentives

Byzantine churches were plain
without and resplendent inside
with coloured marbles, mosaics
and wall-paintings

many Italian cities

1000   1200   1500

ROMANESQUE   GOTHIC

Western Latin Catholic Church ──────►

The Great Schism 1041

Eastern Greek Orthodox Church ──────►

The Byzantine Empire ends

...tic   Second   1204   1261   Third
...sy   'Golden' Period   Latin   Period   1453
                                occupation

69

EARLY CHRISTIAN

S. Stephano Rotondo
Rome (restored),
A.D. 470

S. Apollinare in Classe, Ravenna
A.D. 534-539

apse

bema

nave

aisle

aisle

narthex

atrium

Basilican church
of S. Peter, Rome
(restored),
A.D. 330.
Pulled down in
the 15th century

Syria,
5th-6th centuries:
churches built of large
stone blocks and
timber roofs

Church, Roueiha (restored),
c. 6th century A.D.

S. Costanza,
Rome,
A.D. 330

Baptistery of
Constantine,
Rome,
A.D. 430-440

Visigothic before the Moslem invasion, with horse-shoe arch
S. Juan de Baños, Cerrato, Spain, c. A.D. 500-713

COMPARATIVE PLANS

plans and sections in black to the same scale |⎯⎯|⎯⎯|⎯⎯| 150

S. Prassede, Rome, 822

S. Clemente, Rome, rebuilt 1084-1108 over a 4th-century church

Carolingian: S. Riquier, nr Abbeville, France (restored in 800)

Early Christian-Romanesque: S. Miniato, Florence, A.D. 1013

Oratory, Germigny-des-Pres, France, A.D. 806

5°

Maria de Naranco Asturia, Spain, A.D. 824-840

Mozarabic, 'Arabized Spanish': S. Miguel de Escalada, León, A.D. 913

Spanish-Romanesque: S. Vicente de Cardona, Catalonia, c. 1024-1040

4°

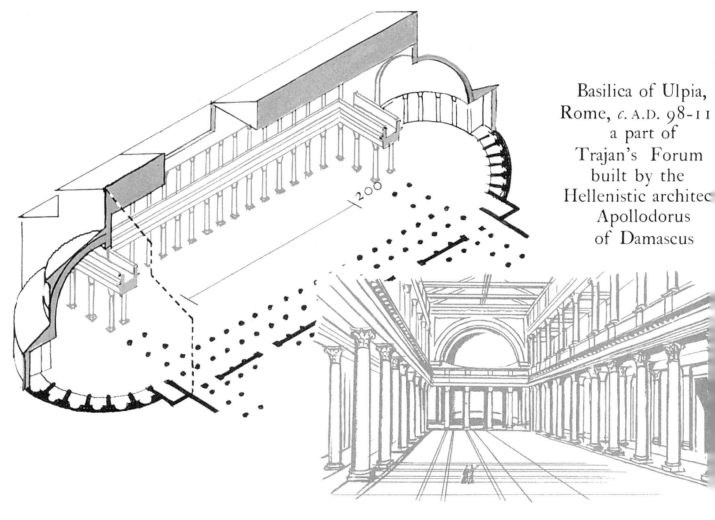

Basilica of Ulpia,
Rome, *c.*A.D. 98-11
a part of
Trajan's Forum
built by the
Hellenistic architec
Apollodorus
of Damascus

TIMBER ROOFS

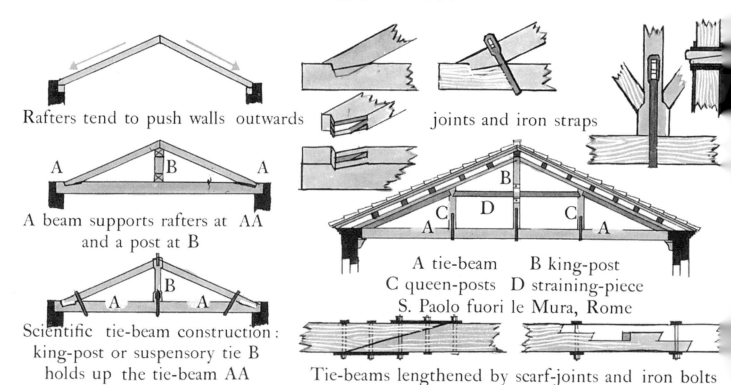

Rafters tend to push walls outwards

joints and iron straps

A beam supports rafters at AA
and a post at B

Scientific tie-beam construction:
king-post or suspensory tie B
holds up the tie-beam AA

A tie-beam   B king-post
C queen-posts D straining-piece
S. Paolo fuori le Mura, Rome

Tie-beams lengthened by scarf-joints and iron bolts

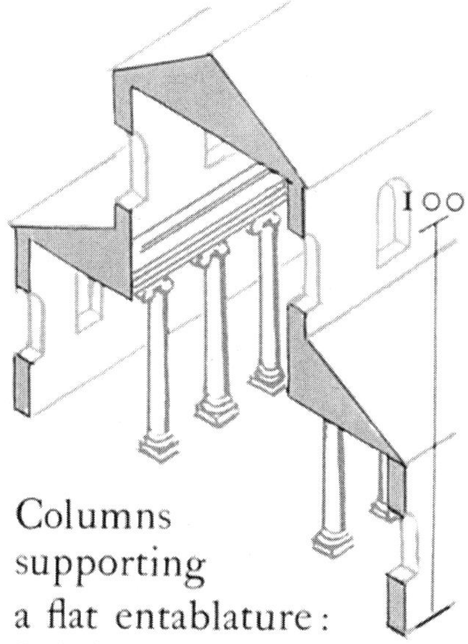

Columns
supporting
a flat entablature:
S. Maria Maggiore,
Rome, A.D. 432

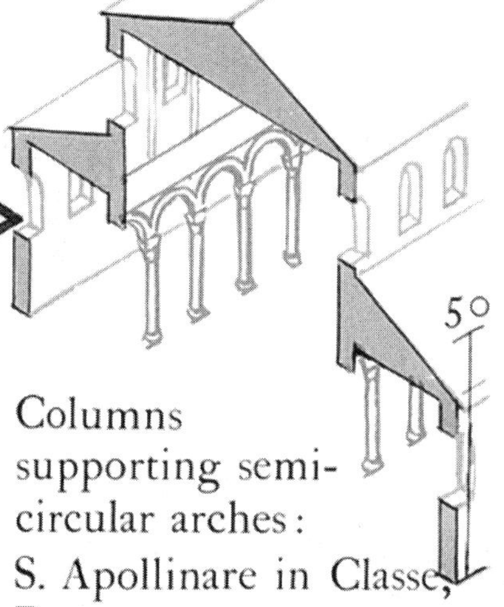

apse

high
altar
bema

nave

aisle

aisle

200

atrium

narthex

100

Columns
supporting semi-
circular arches:
S. Apollinare in Classe,
Ravenna, A.D. 534-539

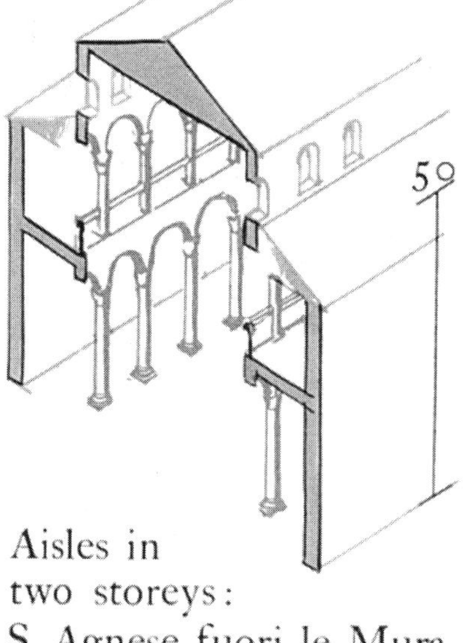

50

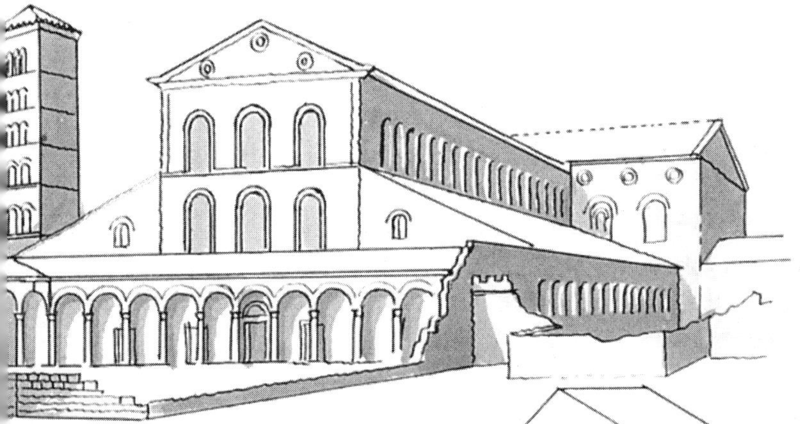

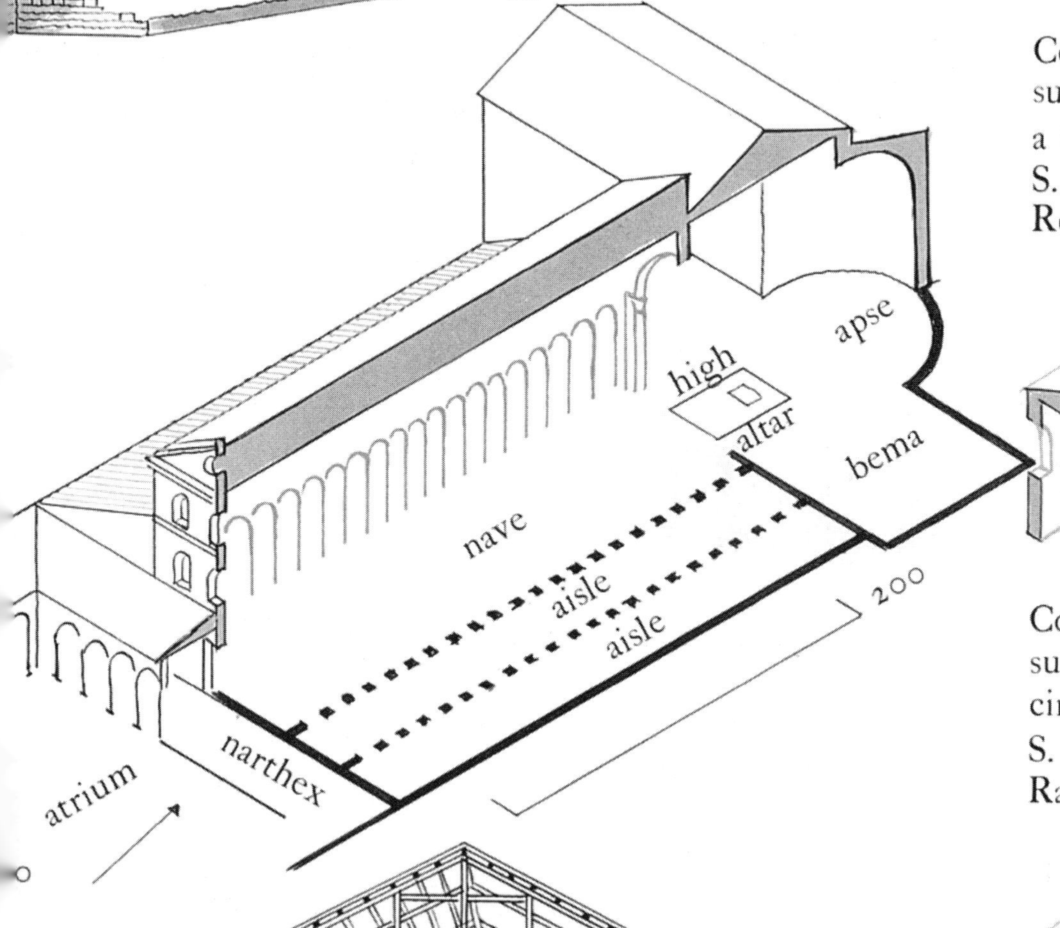

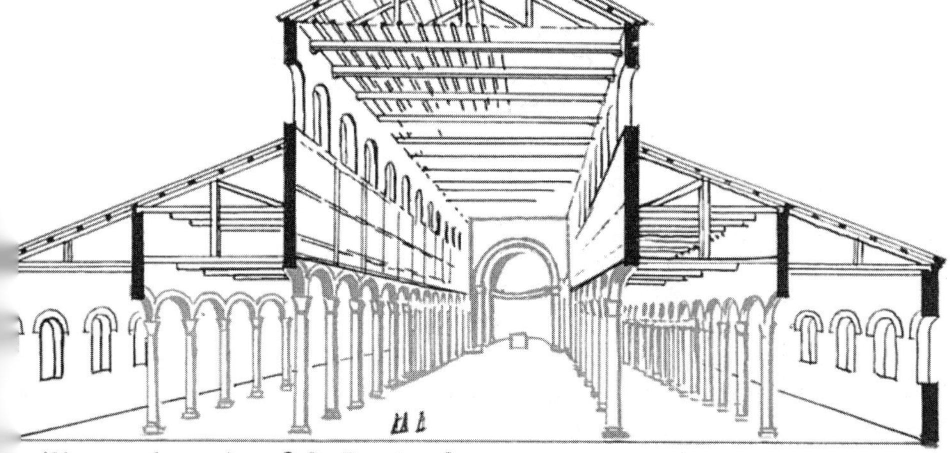

asilican church of S. Paolo fuori le Mura, Rome, A.D. 320;
burnt down in 1832 and rebuilt to the original design

Aisles in
two storeys:
S. Agnese fuori le Mura,
Rome, A.D. 625-638

59

BYZANTINE

ROMAN

The Minerva Medica,
Rome, *c.*A.D. 260

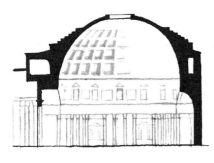

The Pantheon, Rome,
A.D. 120-124

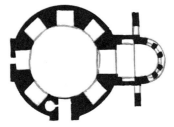

S. George, Salonika,
*c.*A.D. 400

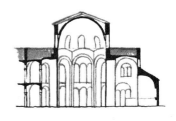

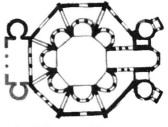

S. Vitale, Ravenna,
A.D. 526-547

SS. Sergius
and Bacchus
Constantinople
A.D. 527-553

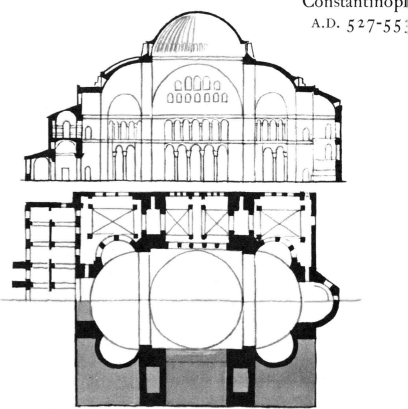

S. Sophia, Constantinople, A.D. 532-537

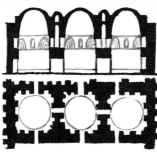

PERSIA:
detail of Palace,
Feruz-abad,
A.D. 450

SYRIA:
S. George,
Ezra,
*c.*A.D. 510

COMPARATIVE PLANS

plans and sections in black to the same scale ⊢——⊣——⊣ 150

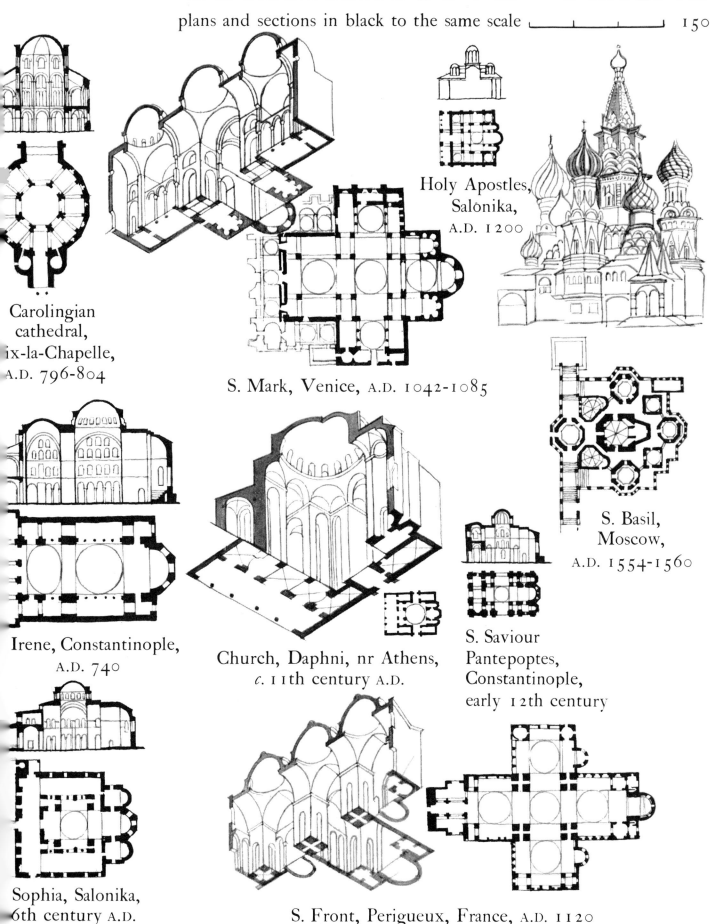

Carolingian
cathedral,
ix-la-Chapelle,
A.D. 796-804

S. Mark, Venice, A.D. 1042-1085

Holy Apostles,
Salonika,
A.D. 1200

S. Basil,
Moscow,
A.D. 1554-1560

Irene, Constantinople,
A.D. 740

Church, Daphni, nr Athens,
c. 11th century A.D.

S. Saviour
Pantepoptes,
Constantinople,
early 12th century

Sophia, Salonika,
6th century A.D.

S. Front, Perigueux, France, A.D. 1120

EARLY CHRISTIAN

The Mausoleum of S. Costanza, Rome, built by Constantine, c. A.D. 324-329.
The dome constructed of concrete with brick ribs and set on a drum supported upon
12 coupled granite columns, the thrust neutralized by the barrel vault of the circular aisl

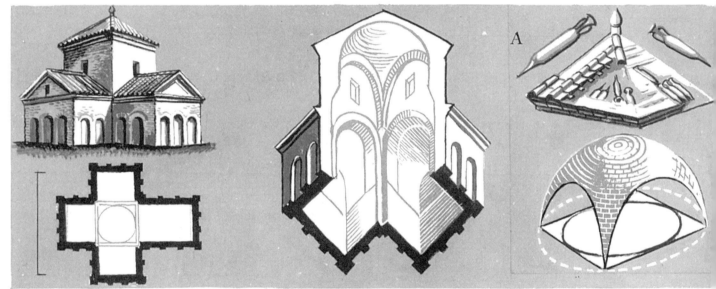

The Tomb of Galla Placidia, Ravenna, c. A.D. 420
An early cruciform plan with a dome and pendentives forming the same hemisphere, o
concentric courses of brick; filling-in of amphorae set in mortar A; mosaics line the inter

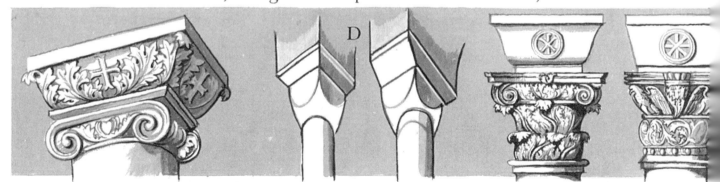

Capitals: S. Demetrius, Salonika, 5th century A.D.

For capitals Roman Ionic, Corinthian and Composite types were used, and a cubiform ty
was evolved, carrying a dosseret block D to support wide voussoirs of arches or thick w

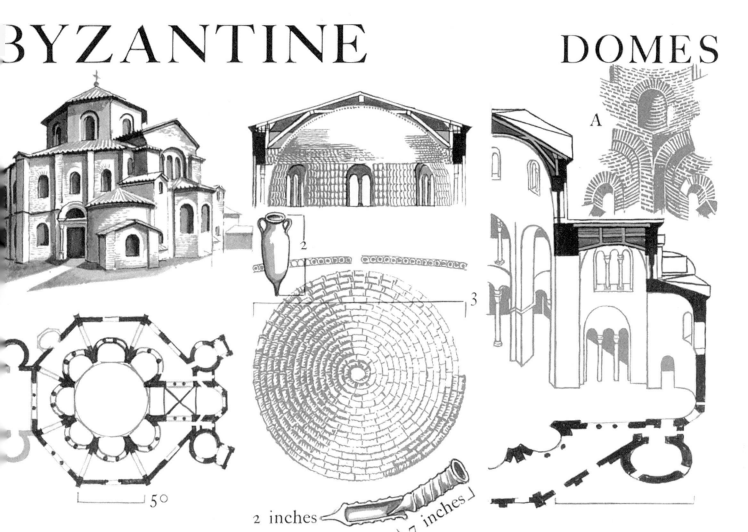

S. Vitale, Ravenna, A.D. 526-547

Founded by Justinian to commemorate the recovery of Ravenna. Built of brick; the dome constructed of terracotta jars embedded in mortar which produced a lightness of structure. The transition of the octagonal space into the circular dome was made by angle-niches A; the lateral thrust of the dome was resisted by the 7 semicircular recesses, the cross-vault of the choir and the butresses on the external walls. The only mosaics not destroyed are in the choir and apse

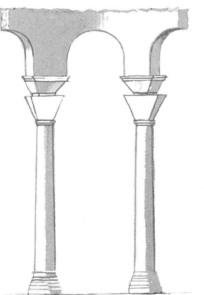

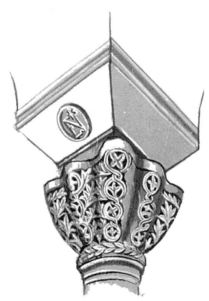

BYZANTINE

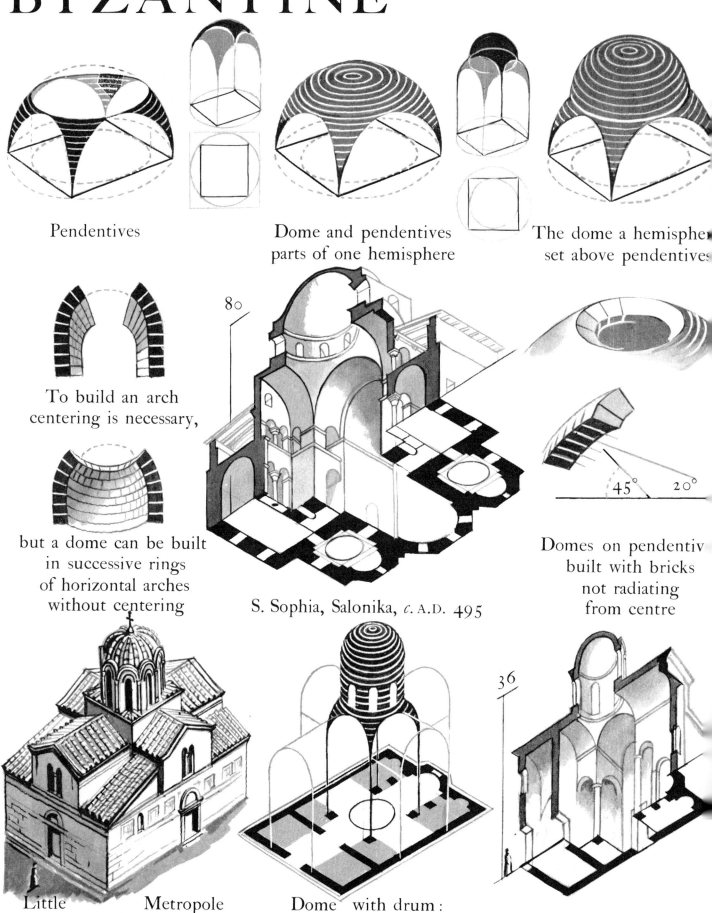

Pendentives

Dome and pendentives parts of one hemisphere

The dome a hemispher set above pendentive

80

To build an arch centering is necessary,

but a dome can be built in successive rings of horizontal arches without centering

S. Sophia, Salonika, *c.* A.D. 495

45° 20°

Domes on pendentiv built with bricks not radiating from centre

36

Little Cathedral,   Metropole Athens, A.D. 1250

Dome with drum: cross-in-square plan

DOMES ON PENDENTIVES

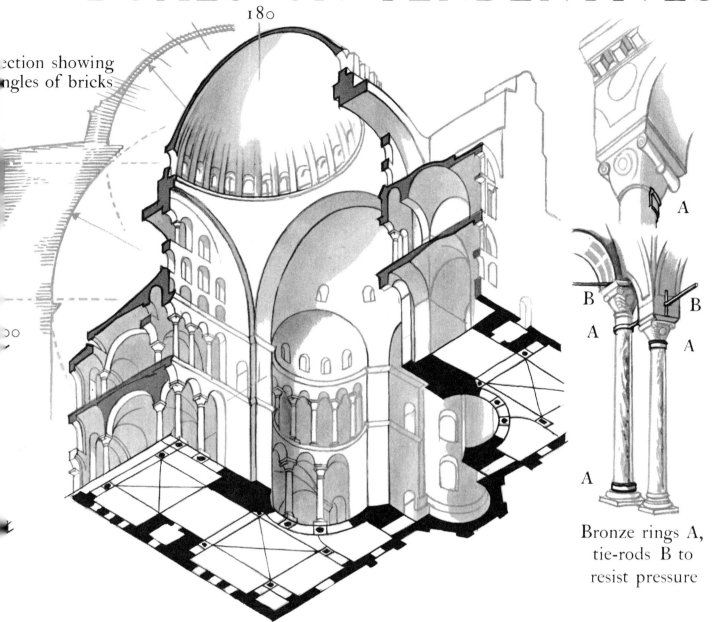

ction showing
ngles of bricks

180

100

A

B   B

A

A

A

A

Bronze rings A,
tie-rods B to
resist pressure

S. Sophia (Hagia Sophia = divine wisdom), Constantinople, A.D. 532-537 (plan p.74)

uilt for Justinian by two Greek
rchitects, Anthemius of Tralles
d Isodorus of Miletus. Built of
ick; the dome probably erected
without centering, with bricks
about 24-27 inches square and
inches thick laid in deep mortar
and covered with $\frac{1}{4}$ inch lead;
e dome supported on 4 piers,
e thrust being taken by 2 semi-
omes and 4 massive buttresses;
e interior lined throughout in
oloured marbles and mosaics

100

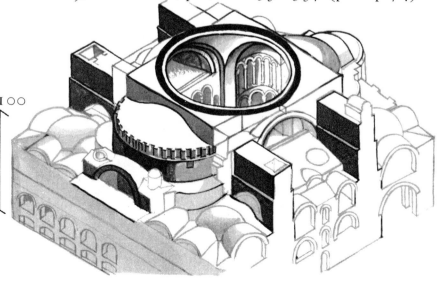

ROMANESQUE

Lindisfarne

*Anglo-Saxon
period
449-1066
Norman
period
1066-1154*

Durham

Fountains · York

Chester · Lincoln

Peterborough · Norwich
Worcester · Ely
Tewkesbury
Gloucester · St Albans
Winchester · Rochester
Exeter · Romsey · Canterbury

GERMANY

French
architectural
regions:

Hildesheim
Gernrode
Cologne · Fulda
Maria Laach
Mainz · RHINE
Worms · LAND
Speyer
Strasbourg

I Normandy
II Anjou
III Poitou
IV Aquitaine
V Auvergne
VI Languedoc
VII Provence
VIII Burgundy

Aix-la-Chapelle
S. Riquier
Bayeux · Jumièges · Prémontré
Caen I · Rouen · Laon
Mont-S. Michel · Paris · S. Denis
Chartres
Orleans · Clairvaux · Vignory
Angers · Germigny-des-Prés
II · Tours
III
Poitiers
Reichenau
S. Gall

Limoges Cluny · Autun
Angoulême · V VIII · LOMBARDY
Soulac · IV · Clermont-Ferrand · Verona · Torcello
Périgueux · Grenoble Milan · Venice
Bordeaux · Le Puy · Pavia
Cahors · Conques
Moissac · VI · VII · Bologna · Ravenna · Zara
S. Sebastian · Toulouse · Arles · Pisa · Florence
Vitoria · Roncesvalles · Assisi
Burgos · ITALY

SPAIN · Rome
Monte Cassino · Traini
Troja · Bar
APULIA

Luco · Oviedo · Le Puy
Santiago · Leon · S. Sebastian
de Compostela · Vitoria · Toulouse
Burgos · Roncesvalles · Palermo · Cefalu
Puente-la-Reina · Monreale
Ripoll · SICILY
SPAIN

Pilgrimage routes to
Santiago de Compostela
principal routes ▬▬▬ **other routes** ▬ ▬ ▬

⊢——⊣ 100 miles

INTRODUCTION

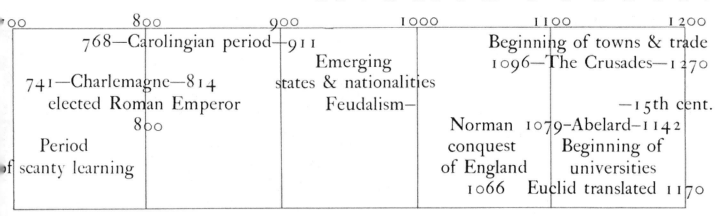

700	800	900	1000	1100	1200
	768—Carolingian period—911			Beginning of towns & trade	
	741—Charlemagne—814	Emerging states & nationalities		1096—The Crusades—1270	
	elected Roman Emperor 800	Feudalism—			—15th cent.
	Period		Norman	1079–Abelard–1142	
of scanty learning			conquest of England 1066	Beginning of universities Euclid translated 1170	

Romanesque architecture (8th-12th centuries) was based on the Roman system of arched buildings, Early Christian basilicas & influences from Syria and Byzantium. In the 10th and 11th centuries both the omnipotence of the Roman Church as a spiritual & a secular power, and the foundation and expansion of the Monastic Orders, resulted in the building of innumerable abbeys, priories, cathedrals and pilgrimage churches. S. Benedict had founded the Benedictines (529), and monks of this Order founded at Cluny the reformed Cluniac Order (910) which pursued the ideal of an united Christendom. At its zenith the 'congregation of Cluny' numbered 1450 monastic houses; followed by the more austere Order of Cistercians founded at Citeaux (1092), which, by 1200, had 694 monasteries. Other Monastic and Military Orders were instituted, followed by the Friars in the early 13th century. The Norman conquest of England (1066) brought a rapid building of abbeys, priories, cathedrals; smaller churches (p.102) & castles (p.104). Few civil buildings remain. Romanesque churches were massive in construction, with thick walls built of smallish stones & rubble, of brick and, in Italy, of marble; they had round arches & small windows, whilst simple columns were transformed into clustered piers. Stone vaulting was developed from the dark barrel-vault to the groined cross-vault, which gave light from clerestory windows. These vaults were built as a protection against fire and as an aid to acoustics.
Ribbed cross-vaults were first constructed at S. Ambrogio, Milan, and in Durham Cathedral in the early 12th century.

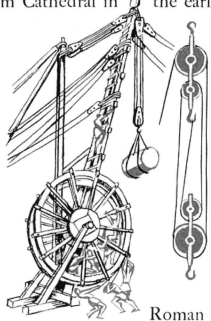

Roman

ROMANESQUE

plans and elevations
to the same scale

|⸻⸻⸻⸻| 200

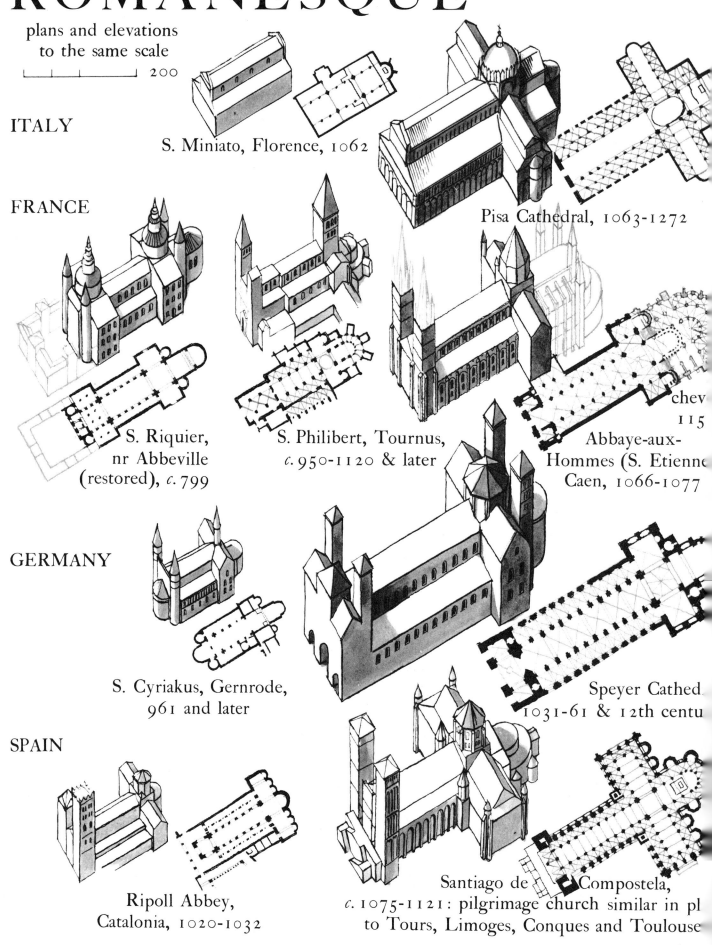

ITALY

S. Miniato, Florence, 1062

Pisa Cathedral, 1063-1272

FRANCE

S. Riquier,
nr Abbeville
(restored), *c.* 799

S. Philibert, Tournus,
c. 950-1120 & later

chev
115
Abbaye-aux-
Hommes (S. Etienne
Caen, 1066-1077

GERMANY

S. Cyriakus, Gernrode,
961 and later

Speyer Cathed
1031-61 & 12th centu

SPAIN

Ripoll Abbey,
Catalonia, 1020-1032

Santiago de   Compostela,
c. 1075-1121: pilgrimage church similar in pl
to Tours, Limoges, Conques and Toulouse

PLANS & ELEVATIONS

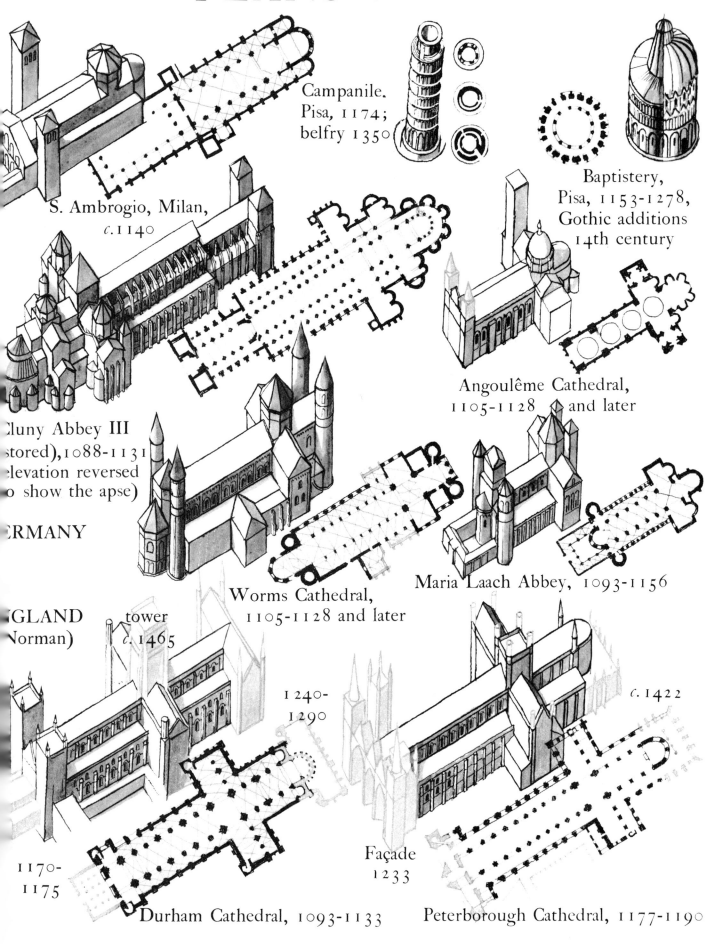

Campanile, Pisa, 1174; belfry 1350

Baptistery, Pisa, 1153-1278, Gothic additions 14th century

S. Ambrogio, Milan, c.1140

Cluny Abbey III (restored), 1088-1131 (elevation reversed to show the apse)

GERMANY

Angoulême Cathedral, 1105-1128 and later

Worms Cathedral, 1105-1128 and later

Maria Laach Abbey, 1093-1156

ENGLAND (Norman)

tower c.1465

1240-1290

c.1422

1170-1175

Façade 1233

Durham Cathedral, 1093-1133

Peterborough Cathedral, 1177-1190

ROMANESQUE

S. Miniato,
Florence, 1013

Pisa Cathedral,
1063-1092

Troja Cathedral,
begun 1093

S. Zeno, Veron
c. 1123-1135

Hildesheim
1001-1033

Jumièges,
1037-1066

S. Trinité, Caen,
1062-1140

S. Germain-des-Pré
Paris, c. 1160

Notre-Dame-la-Grande,
Poitiers, 1130-1145

Tewkesbury Abbey,
c. 1150

Celafù Cathedral,
1131-1200

84

2 orders with label

omanesque
orders

Roman
order

billet
nail-head
cable
chevron
bowtell

concentric orders
built on light centering

Cubiform capitals

Corinthian capitals

ribs related to
a circular column
and clustered pier

ROMANESQUE

scale for
sections
5°

BARREL VAULTS

GROINED VAULT

S. Savin-sur-Gartempe,
c. 1060-1115

S. Sernin, Toulouse,
1080-1096

S. Madelaine, Vézela
c. 1104-1132

centering
of
mounded
earth

timber
centering

wedges

groin stones
1,2 joint moulds
1a, 2b plans

1

1a

2

2b 2

STONE VAULTING

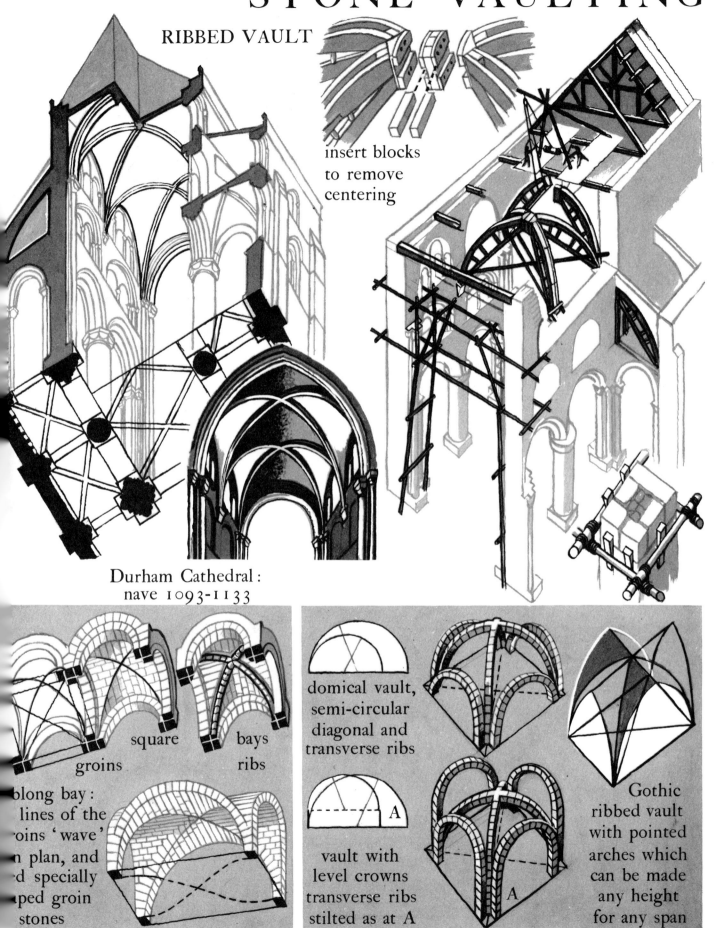

RIBBED VAULT

insert blocks
to remove
centering

Durham Cathedral:
nave 1093-1133

square   bays
groins   ribs

blong bay:
lines of the
oins 'wave'
n plan, and
d specially
ped groin
stones

domical vault,
semi-circular
diagonal and
transverse ribs

vault with
level crowns
transverse ribs
stilted as at A

Gothic
ribbed vault
with pointed
arches which
can be made
any height
for any span

ROMANESQUE

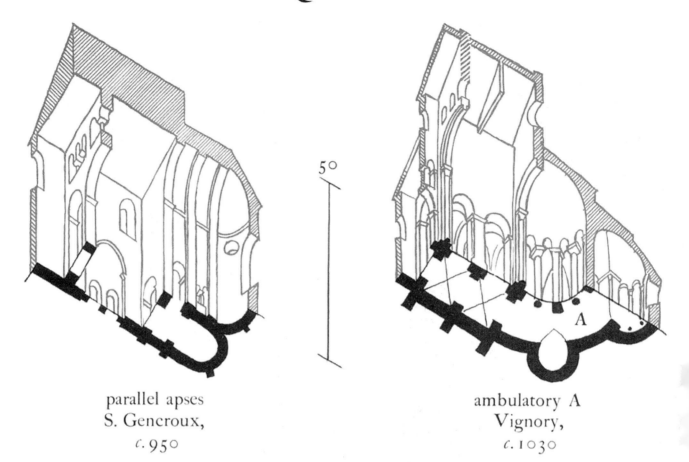

parallel apses
S. Generoux,
c. 950

5°

ambulatory A
Vignory,
c. 1030

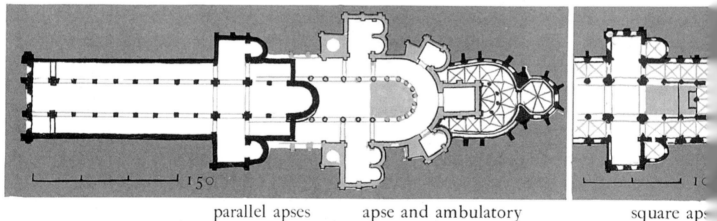

parallel apses   apse and ambulatory   square aps

1070-1077   1096-1130   1174-1184   *c*. 1120

Canterbury Cathedral   Romsey Abbey

150   10

The plan of the Romanesque church was based on that of the Early Christian basilica, b
prominence was given to the transepts, choir and apse. In addition to parallel apses the
was an ambulatory with radiating chapels called a Chevet (Fr. chef = head). An increase
the veneration of saints & sacred relics and in the numbers of pilgrims resulted in the ne
for the ambulatory or processional way. The Chevet became the typical form of east e
for churches in Northern France. In England, e.g. at Canterbury and Norwich, it gav
way to a square ending.

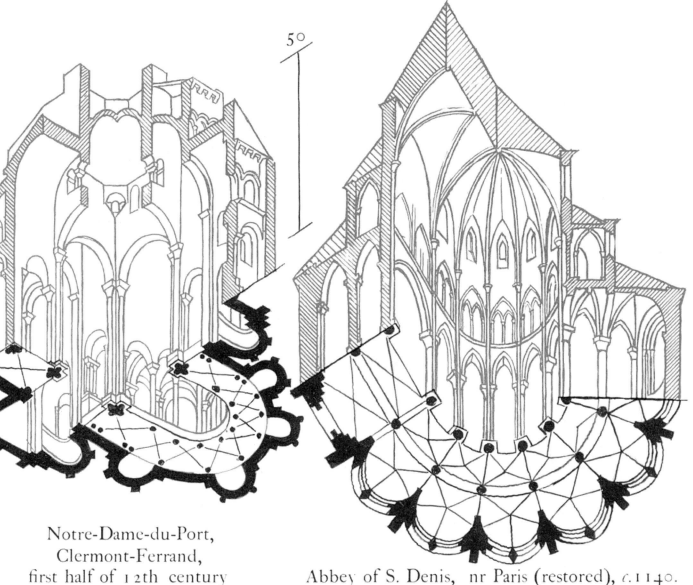

5°

Notre-Dame-du-Port,
Clermont-Ferrand,
first half of 12th century

Abbey of S. Denis, nr Paris (restored), c.1140.
Built by Abbot Suger (1122-1151),
who 'enlarged and amplified the noble church'
because of the 'narrowness of the place'.

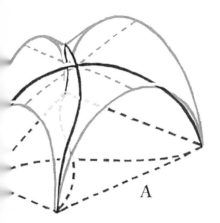

A

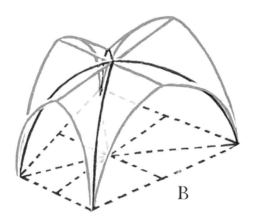

B

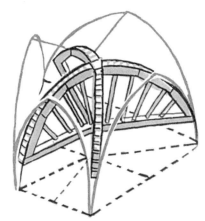

In ambulatory bays curved groins, made by the intersection of barrel-vaults A,
were simplified and strengthened by the introduction of the Gothic pointed arch B

GOTHIC

Edinburgh

Armagh Carlisle Durham

Ripon

York

Conway Chester

Harlech Lincoln

Lichfield

Gloucester Ely Peterborough

Oxford Cambridge

Winchester London

Exeter Canterbury

English Architectural Periods
Norman: late 11th & 12th
  centuries
Early English: 13th century
Decorated: 14th century
Perpendicular: 15th century

Brick Gothic

Lübeck Chorin

Bremen

Utrecht

Münster 'Hall' Churches

Bruges Cologne

Ghent Antwerp

Amiens Marburg Annaberg

French
Architectural
Periods

Rouen Beauvais Laon Limburg Prague

S. Denis Rheims Oppenheim

Gothique à
Lancettes:
12th century

Chartres Paris Dinkelsbühl Nuremberg

Orléans Troyes Strasbourg Augsburg Vienna

Angers Sens Freiburg Ulm Munich

Rayonnant:
13th century

Bourges Citeaux Salzburg

Poitiers Cluny

Flamboyant:
14th, 15th
& early
16th centuries

Clermont

Milan Verona Venice

Padua

Bordeaux

Bologna

Single-nave Genoa
Churches Albi Avignon

Toulouse Arles Pisa Florence

Burgos Siena Perugia

Carcassonne Orvieto Assisi

Gerona Rome

Barcelona

Naples

Santiago

León Burgos

Barcelona

Avila Segovia Palermo

Toledo Monreale Messina

Valencia

100 miles

c.1212

c.1230

c.1475

The retreat *of the Moors*

100 miles

INTRODUCTION

100	1200	1300	1400	1500 1550
Increase of trade, growth of towns, & rise of guilds	Ascension of Gothic in Ile de France	Black Death 1348-49 1346-The 100 Years' War-1453		1453 End of Eastern Byzantine Empire
Universities Aristotle (via Arabs)	Scholasticism c.1225–S. Aquinas–c.1275	Humanism 1304-Petrarch-1374 1265–Dante-1321	Italian RENAISSANCE	1452–Leonardo da Vinci –1519
Discoveries: 1214-Roger Bacon-1294 optical lens, mariner's compass, gunpowder, cannon			c.1450 printing	

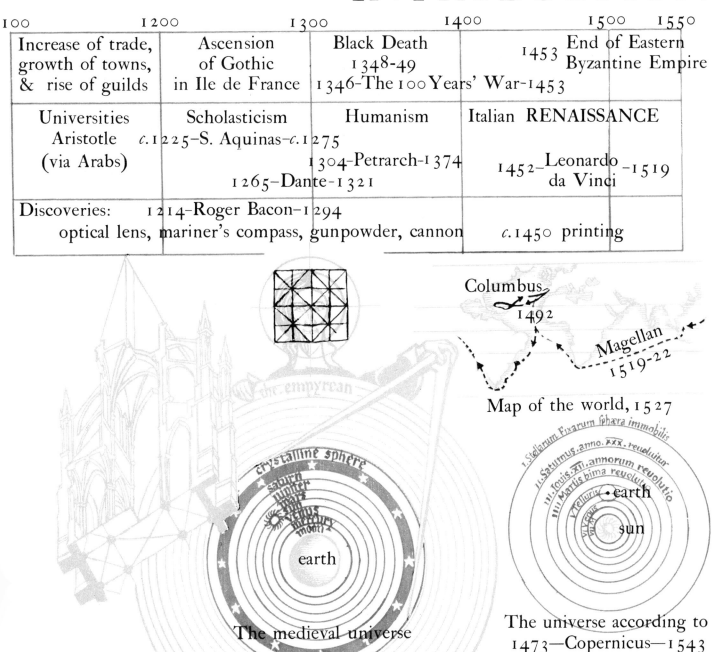

Columbus 1492

Magellan 1519-22

Map of the world, 1527

The medieval universe

The universe according to 1473—Copernicus—1543

The enlargement of S. Denis, 1144 (p.89) inaugurated a lyrical form of construction in which pointed arches, high stone vaults and flying buttresses were fused into an organic whole, and which reached a crescendo in the cathedrals built in the Ile de France (pp.100-01). Gothic, or the 'style Ogivale' (Fr.: pointed) was known as 'Opus Modernum' or 'Opus Francigenum' (French work); the term 'Gothic', i.e. barbarian, was first used by the Humanists of the Renaissance. Few plans survive by the lay master-masons, who designed their buildings with 'a good wit of geometry' and who directed the quarry-men, stone-cutters, smiths, carpenters & workmen. In England (pp.102-105), France (pp.106-107), Italy (pp.108-109) and Germany (pp.110-111) castles, parish churches, guild-halls and houses followed the same pattern of pointed arches, pinnacles, spires & high-pitched roofs. South of the Alps in Italy Gothic was neutralised by the Roman tradition and ceased with the advent of the Renaissance in the 15th century.

GOTHIC

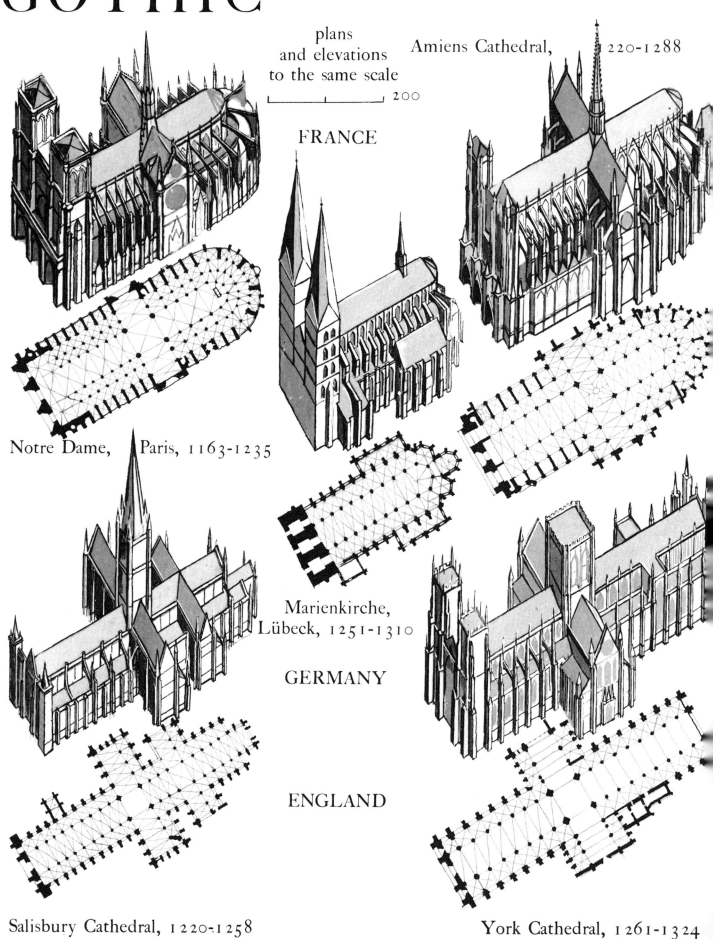

plans
and elevations
to the same scale

|————————| 200

Amiens Cathedral, 220-1288

FRANCE

Notre Dame, Paris, 1163-1235

Marienkirche,
Lübeck, 1251-1310

GERMANY

ENGLAND

Salisbury Cathedral, 1220-1258

York Cathedral, 1261-1324

PLANS & ELEVATIONS

ITALY

Florence Cathedral, 1296-1462

dome added by Brunelleschi 1420-37

three apses completed 1421

Siena Cathedral, 1245-1380

SPAIN

Burgos Cathedral, 1220-1500

St Peter's, Rome, begun 1506

GOTHIC

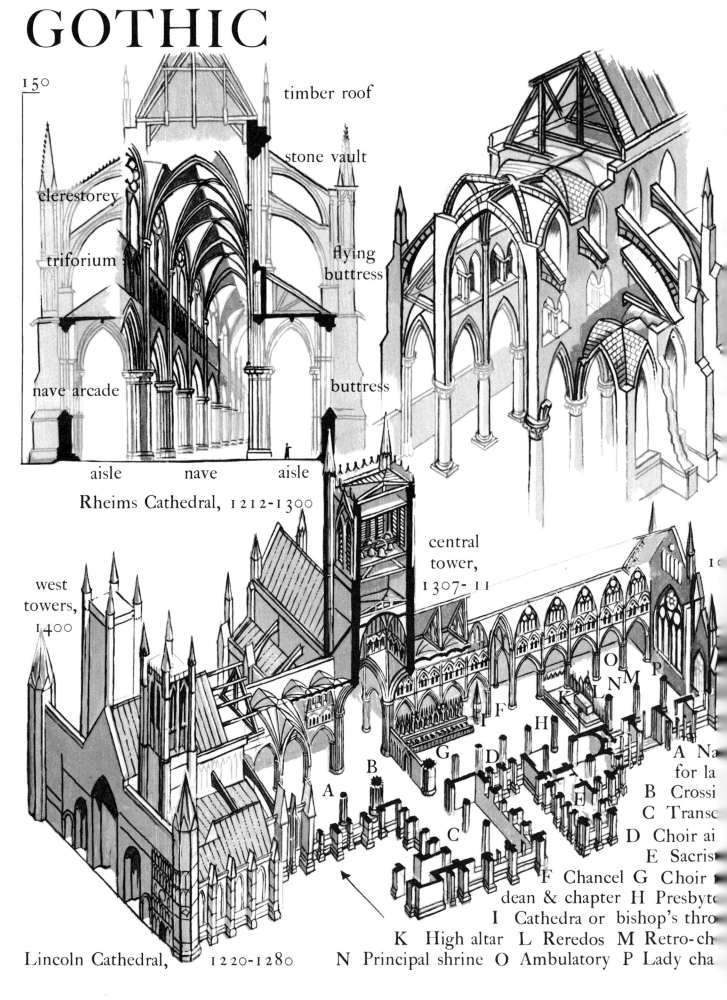

150

timber roof

stone vault

clerestorey

triforium

flying
buttress

nave arcade

buttress

aisle   nave   aisle

Rheims Cathedral, 1212-1300

west
towers,
1400

central
tower,
1307-11

A
B
C
D
E
F
G
H
K
L
M
N
O
P

A Na
   for la
B Crossi
C Transe
D Choir ai
E Sacris
F Chancel G Choir
dean & chapter H Presbyt
I Cathedra or bishop's thro
K High altar L Reredos M Retro-ch
N Principal shrine O Ambulatory P Lady cha

Lincoln Cathedral,   1220-1280

THE PARTS OF A CATHEDRAL

Laon Cathedral,
c. 1235

Notre Dame, Paris,
c. 1200-1250

Rheims Cathedral,
c. 1255-c. 1290

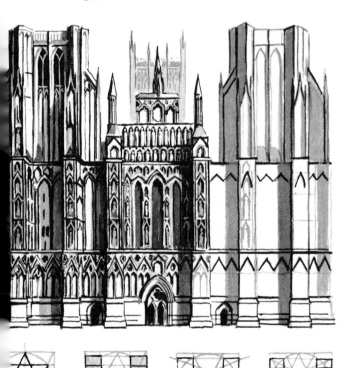

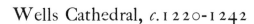

Wells Cathedral, c. 1220-1242   Peterborough Cathedral, c. 1235

THE WEST FRONT

GOTHIC

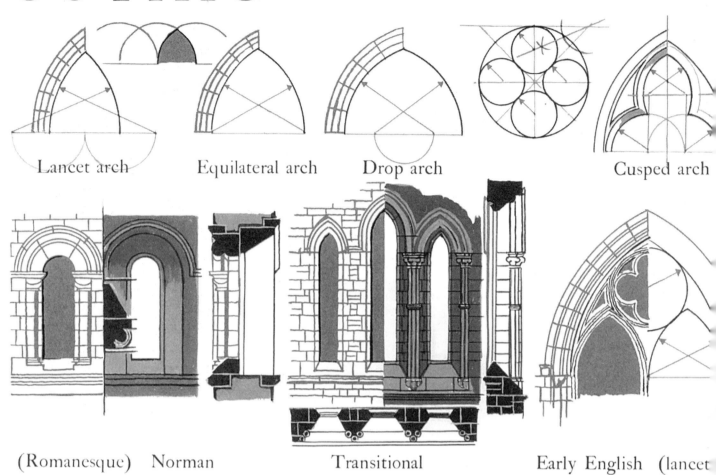

Lancet arch   Equilateral arch   Drop arch   Cusped arch

(Romanesque) Norman   Transitional   Early English (lancet

Peterborough Cathedral: Ripon Cathedral: Ely Cathedral:
choir, *c.*1140   choir, 1154-1181   presbytery, 1235-125

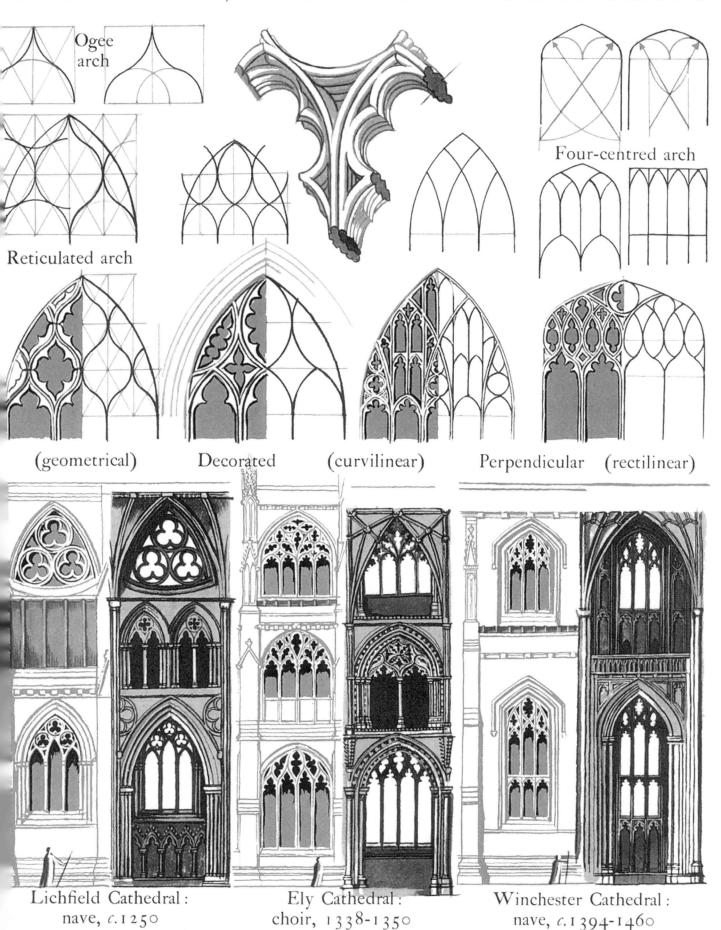

Ogee arch

Four-centred arch

Reticulated arch

(geometrical)　　Decorated　　(curvilinear)　　Perpendicular　(rectilinear)

Lichfield Cathedral:
nave, c.1250

Ely Cathedral:
choir, 1338-1350

Winchester Cathedral:
nave, c.1394-1460

GOTHIC

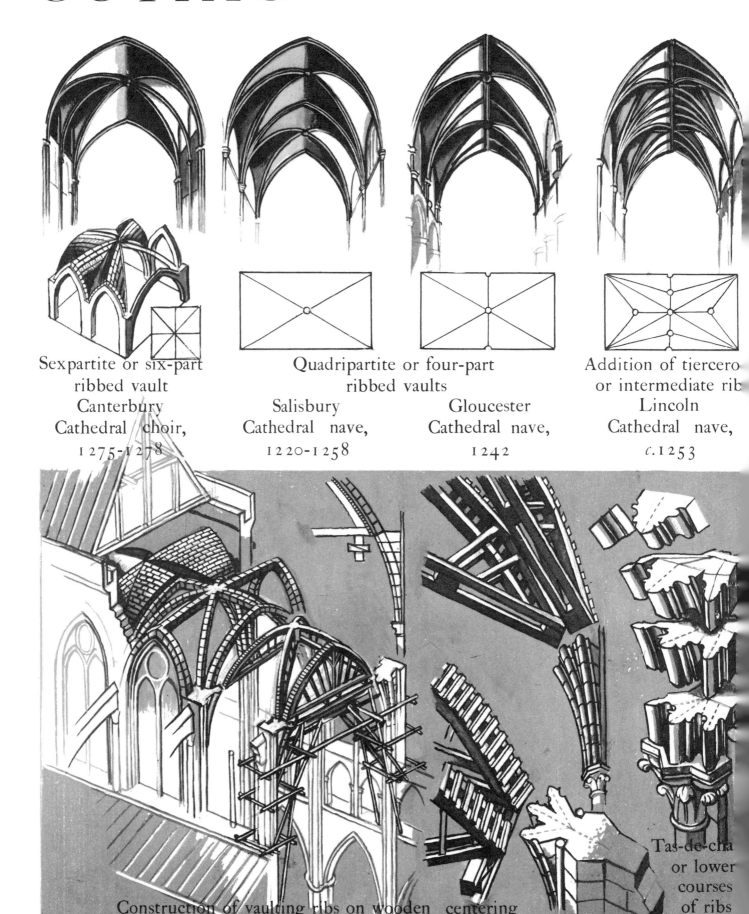

Sexpartite or six-part
ribbed vault
Canterbury
Cathedral choir,
1275-1278

Quadripartite or four-part
ribbed vaults
Salisbury
Cathedral nave,
1220-1258

Gloucester
Cathedral nave,
1242

Addition of tiercero
or intermediate rib
Lincoln
Cathedral nave,
c.1253

Construction of vaulting ribs on wooden centering

Tas-de-cha
or lower
courses
of ribs

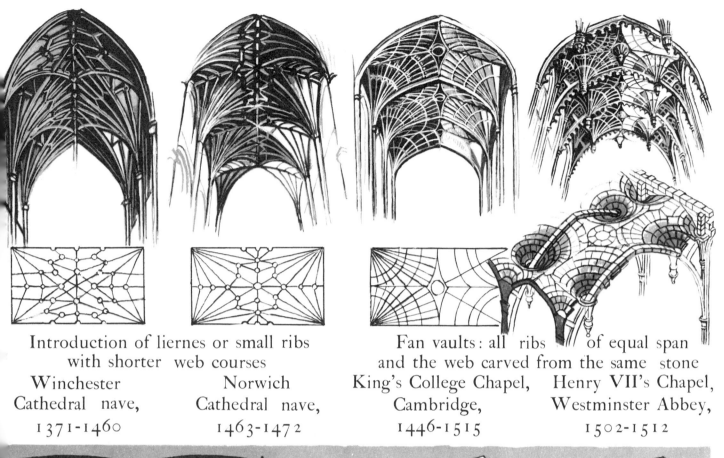

Introduction of liernes or small ribs
with shorter web courses

Winchester Cathedral nave, 1371-1460	Norwich Cathedral nave, 1463-1472

Fan vaults: all ribs of equal span
and the web carved from the same stone

King's College Chapel, Cambridge, 1446-1515	Henry VII's Chapel, Westminster Abbey, 1502-1512

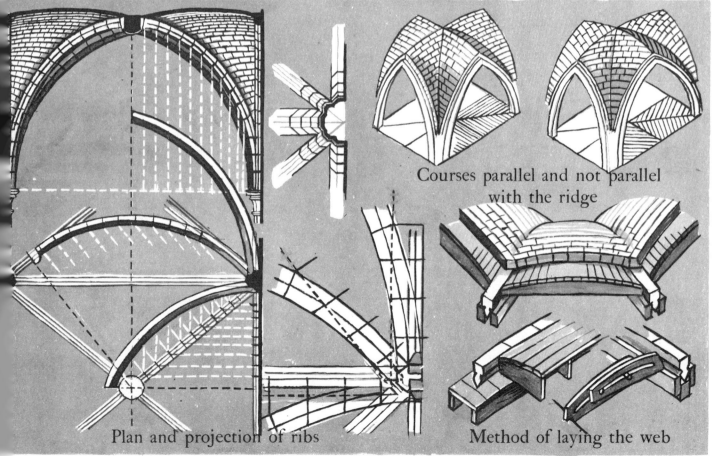

Courses parallel and not parallel
with the ridge

Plan and projection of ribs

Method of laying the web

GOTHIC CATHEDRALS

100

200

100

Noyon, c.1150-55   Notre Dame, Paris, 1163-1235   Chartres,

94-1260   Amiens, 1220-88   Beauvais, 1225-72

projected
nave

GOTHIC

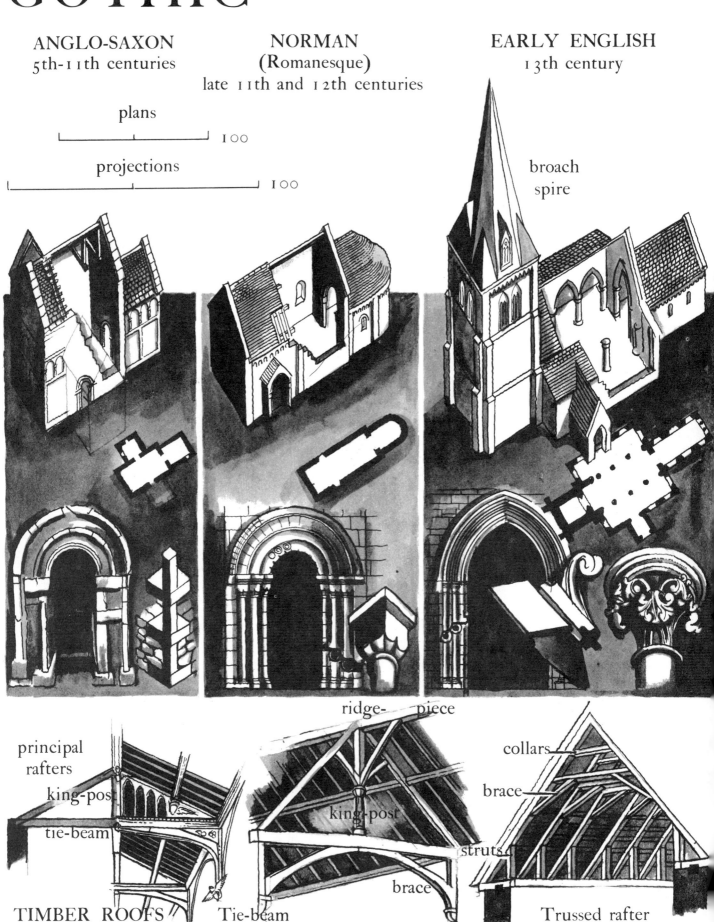

ANGLO-SAXON
5th-11th centuries

NORMAN
(Romanesque)
late 11th and 12th centuries

EARLY ENGLISH
13th century

plans

100

projections

100

broach
spire

principal
rafters

king-post

tie-beam

ridge-
piece

king-post

brace

collars

brace

struts

brace

TIMBER ROOFS

Tie-beam

Trussed rafter

ENGLAND, THE PARISH CHURCH

DECORATED
14th century

PERPENDICULAR
15th century

Collar-braced   Hammer-beam   Hammer-beam

GOTHIC

Norman motte-&-bailey castle
(reconstructed), 11th century

Shell keep and bailey
(reconstructed), early 12th century

Section of a square keep,
early 12th century

Castle Hedingham, Essex, c.1140

Orford, Suffolk, c.1165-7

Conisborough, Yorkshire c.1170

Square to round keep

The Manor House,
Boothby Pagnall, Lincolnshire, c.1180

1st floor
hall
chapel

chapel

Little Wenham Hall,
Suffolk, c.1260-1286

Conway, Caernarvonshire, 1283-1287, built by Edward I

outer bailey

inner bailey

barbican

gateway & barbican

hall

200

concentric plan

200

Harlech, Merionethshire, 1283-1289, built by Edward I

2nd-floor

ground-floor

5°

The decline of the castle Tattershall, Lincolnshire: tower-house of brick, 1434-1446

chamber, solar above

dais

hall

screen

hearth

buttery

5°

Penshurst Place, Kent, c.1341

solar

5°

buttery

pantry

hall

chamber, solar above

Cothay Manor, Somerset, c.1480

GOTHIC

Town houses, stone & brick, *c.*13th century
S. Antonin   Caussade

Town houses, half-timbered, *c.*13th century
Châteaudun   Rouen

main
hall

section of donjon or keep

Château de Courcy (restored), 13th century

spiral staircase   drawbridge and portcullis

5°

150

The house of Jacques Cœur, Bourges, 1443

kitchen

Château de Saumur,
from *Les très riches heures du
Duc de Berry*, by Pol de
Limbourg, *c.*1409-1416

Château de Pierrefonds (restored),
*c.*1390

merlon

rampart

crenel or
opening

crenellation or embattlement

Enfilade

Machicolation, wooden hoarding

GOTHIC

NORTH ITALY

Milan Cathedral,
1385-1485,
built by German, French &
Italian master-masons. The sectional
diagram from Caesare Cesariano's edition of
'Vitruvius' (Como, 1521) is based on a design made
in 1391 to establish the heights of the nave and aisles

Palazzo Loredan,
12th century

Palazzo Pisani,
14th century

Details of Venetian palaces on the Grand Canal

c.1309 onwards   c.1423-38

The Palace of the Doges, Venice

CENTRAL ITALY

200

200

275

The storeys appear equal
to a spectator at A

mpanile, Florence, 1334-1387,
designed by Giotto

Method of laying bricks

Florence Cathedral,
1296-1462 (plan p.91),
begun by Arnolfo di Gambio,
and continued by Giotto,
master of works 1334-37,
Andrea Pisano and Talenti,
who enlarged the first plan.
Choir and 3 apses built
1350-1421.
The dome constructed by
Brunelleschi 1420-1437,
in brick without centering.

GOTHIC

38

S. Elizabeth, Marburg, *c.* 1233-1283:
one of the many 'Hall' churches in North Germany,
having the nave and aisles of equal height

Chorin Abbey, *c.* 1273-1334:
west front

Freiburg Cathedral, *c.* 1268-1288:
west front

GERMANY

S. George, Dinkelsbühl, 1448-1492

S. Anna, Annaburg, 1499-1526

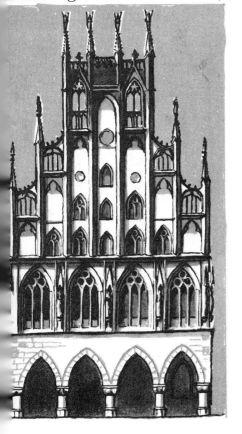

Town hall, Münster,
late 14th century

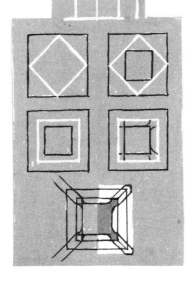

plan & elevation
of a pinnacle after
Roriczer German
master-mason, c.1492

S. Catherine, Oppenheim,
c.1300

RENAISSANCE BAROQUE

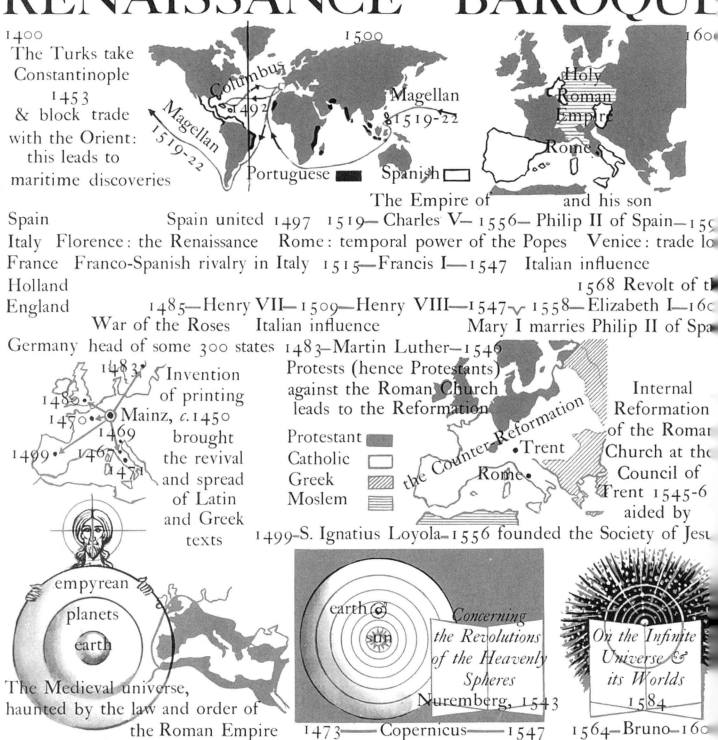

1400

The Turks take Constantinople 1453 & block trade with the Orient: this leads to maritime discoveries

Columbus 1492

Magellan 1519-22

Magellan 1519-22

Portuguese ■ Spanish □

Holy Roman Empire

Rome

The Empire of   and his son

Spain   Spain united 1497 1519— Charles V —1556— Philip II of Spain—159

Italy Florence: the Renaissance   Rome: temporal power of the Popes   Venice: trade lo

France Franco-Spanish rivalry in Italy 1515—Francis I—1547 Italian influence

Holland   1568 Revolt of tl

England   1485—Henry VII—1509—Henry VIII—1547 ⌄ 1558—Elizabeth I—16c

         War of the Roses   Italian influence   Mary I marries Philip II of Spa

Germany head of some 300 states 1483—Martin Luther—1546

1483 Invention of printing Mainz, c.1450 brought the revival and spread of Latin and Greek texts

1486 1450 1469 1499 1467 1470

Protests (hence Protestants) against the Roman Church leads to the Reformation

Protestant ■
Catholic □
Greek ▨
Moslem ▤

the Counter-Reformation

Trent

Rome

Internal Reformation of the Romar Church at the Council of Trent 1545-6 aided by

1499—S. Ignatius Loyola—1556 founded the Society of Jesu

empyrean
planets
earth

The Medieval universe, haunted by the law and order of the Roman Empire

earth
sun

Concerning the Revolutions of the Heavenly Spheres Nuremberg, 1543

1473——Copernicus——1547

On the Infinite Universe & its Worlds 1584

1564—Bruno—16c

THE RENAISSANCE

The Renaissance (Florence)   High Renaissance (Rome) Mannerism

1400   1500   16

Renaissance churches were centralized and designed on the drawing-board.
They were inspired by classical architecture, as interpreted by Vitruvius (above all, by Roman temples, arches, domes & the Five Orders (pp.116-117)), & obeyed the canon

of the Divine Proportions (pp.118-119
The increasingly dramatic movements o
High Renaissance and Mannerist buildin;
became, especially in the 'theatrical' churcl
of the Counter-Reformation, an interpla
of forces. (This required the drawing o

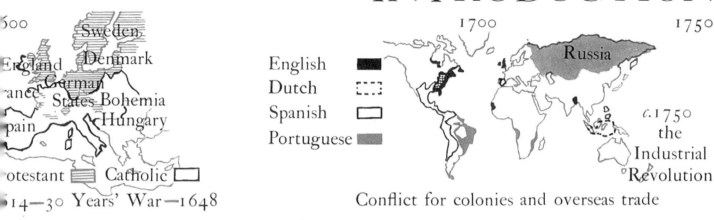

1700   1750

English   ▰
Dutch   ▱
Spanish   ▱
Portuguese ▰

Russia

c.1750
the
Industrial
Revolution

Sweden
Denmark
England German
France States Bohemia
Spain Hungary

Protestant ▤ Catholic ▱

1614—30 Years' War—1648   Conflict for colonies and overseas trade

new Atlantic seaports. Domination of Spain in Italy ends 1710

1610-Age of the Cardinals-1643-Ascension of France: Louis XIV—1715—Louis XV—1774

Netherlands from Spain 1648 Republic of the United Provinces

James I-1625- Charles I-1649⌄1660-Charles II-1685⌄89 1702-Anne-14-George I-1727

Divine Right of Kings   Commonwealth   James II   Colonial Expansion

Impoverished by the 30 Years' War Kingdom of Prussia 1701 Frederick the Great 1740-85

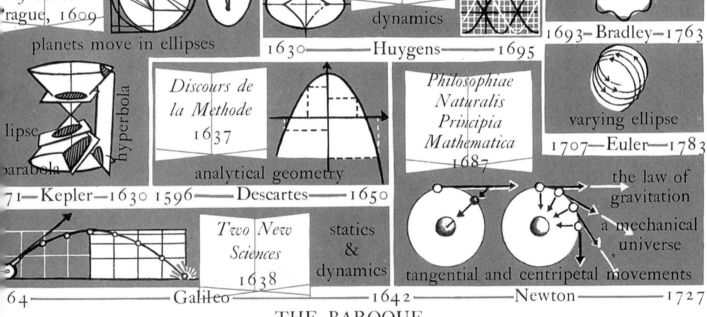

The New Astronomy . . . the Motions of Mars Prague, 1609

planets move in ellipses

Horologium Oscillatorium Paris 1673

dynamics

motions of the earth

undulating

1693—Bradley—1763

1630———Huygens———1695

hyperbola

ellipse

parabola

Discours de la Methode 1637

analytical geometry

Philosophiae Naturalis Principia Mathematica 1687

varying ellipse

1707—Euler—1783

the law of gravitation

a mechanical universe

1571—Kepler—1630 1596———Descartes———1650

Two New Sciences 1638

statics & dynamics

tangential and centripetal movements

1564———Galileo———1642———Newton———1727

THE BAROQUE

Baroque   Rococo

1600   1700   1750

three-dimensional elevations and curved details by means of projective geometry, which had been developed by the new science of dynamics.)
This Baroque style was finally resolved into the lighter curves of the Rococo.

The architecture of each European country was a reaction to that of Italy, modified by its own native characteristics.
France (pp.130-133), Germany & Austria (pp.134-135), Spain (pp.136-137), England (pp.138-159).

RENAISSANCE - BAROQUE

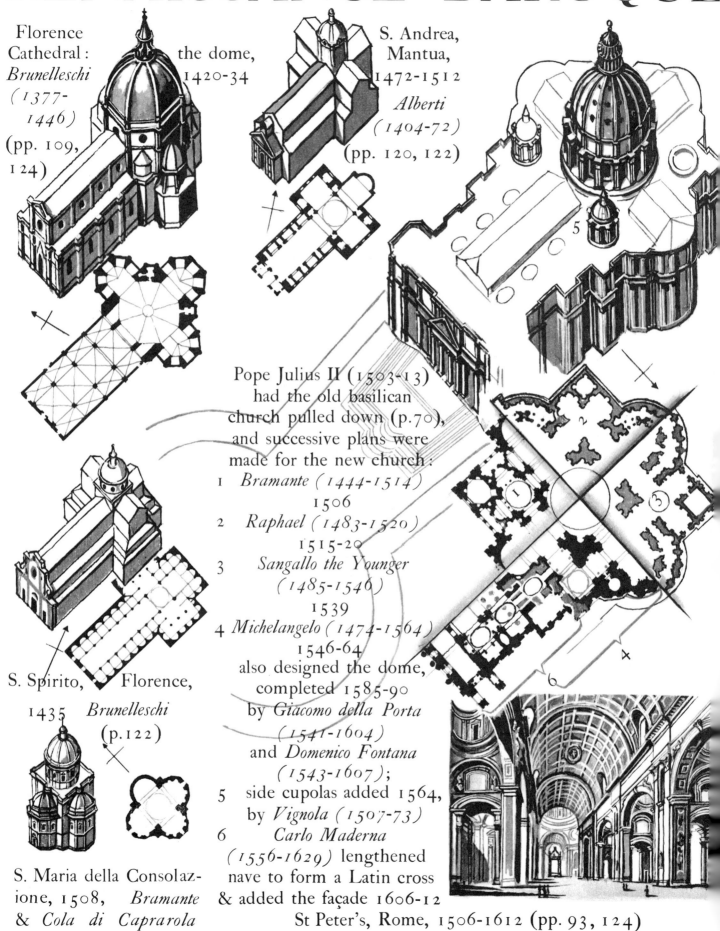

Florence Cathedral: *Brunelleschi* (*1377-1446*) (pp. 109, 124)

the dome, 1420-34

S. Andrea, Mantua, 1472-1512 *Alberti* (*1404-72*) (pp. 120, 122)

S. Spirito, Florence, 1435 *Brunelleschi* (p. 122)

S. Maria della Consolazione, 1508, *Bramante & Cola di Caprarola*

Pope Julius II (1503-13) had the old basilican church pulled down (p.70), and successive plans were made for the new church:

1 *Bramante (1444-1514)* 1506
2 *Raphael (1483-1520)* 1515-20
3 *Sangallo the Younger (1485-1546)* 1539
4 *Michelangelo (1474-1564)* 1546-64
also designed the dome, completed 1585-90 by *Giacomo della Porta (1541-1604)* and *Domenico Fontana (1543-1607)*;
5 side cupolas added 1564, by *Vignola (1507-73)*
6 *Carlo Maderna (1556-1629)* lengthened nave to form a Latin cross & added the façade 1606-12

St Peter's, Rome, 1506-1612 (pp. 93, 124)

PLANS & ELEVATIONS

plans and elevations
to the same scale

500

he Gesù,
Rome,
1568-75
Vignola
(1507-73)
pp. 120,
122)

S. Maria della Salute,
Venice, 1632
Longhena (1604-75)

Piazza, St Peter's, Rome, 1655-67
Bernini (1589-1680)

Vierzehnheiligen,
S. Germany,
1744-72 *Neumann*
(1687-1753)
(p. 137)

he
curial,
near
Madrid,
1559-84

Juan
de Herrara
(c.1530-97)
(p. 138)

he Dome of the Invalides, Paris,
1693-1706   *J. H. Mansart*
646-1708)   (pp. 125, 131)

St Paul's   Cathedral, London,
1675-1710
Sir Christopher Wren (1631-1723)
(pp. 144-145)

Karlskirch,
Vienna,
1716-29
J. B. Fischer
von Erlach
(1656-1725)

from Vignola (1507-1573), *Regola delli Cinque Ordini d'Architettura*, 1562

Doric Order

height of column = 8 diameters, 16 modules

6 12
parts

1 module

Toscane parte ·VI·
Dorica parte ·VII·
Ionita parte ·VIII·
corintha parte ·IX·
composita parte ·X·

The Five Orders, after *Serlio*, 1540

Doric Ionic Corinthian (Pilasters)

Superimposition of Orders:
The Colosseum, Rome, A.D. 70-82

Ionic
$\frac{1}{2}$ 3 4

Composite
$2\frac{1}{2}$ $3\frac{1}{2}$

Corinthian
$\frac{3}{4}$ $2\frac{1}{2}$ $3\frac{2}{3}$

Tuscan
$\frac{3}{4}$ 3 4

Doric
$1\frac{1}{2}$ $2\frac{3}{4}$ 4 $2\frac{3}{4}$

The intercolumnations of each Order, after *Gibbs*, 1732

m 50

m 9

3 6
minutes

1 module

modules 38

2

The Ionic arch with pedestal:
the Colosseum   after *Palladio*, 1570

6 modules

28 modules

1 2 3 modules

9 modules

the Pantheon,
Rome,
A.D. 120-124, & the Basilica
Rome,

of Constantine

A.D. 310-313

after *Serlio* (Bk I), 1545

after *Gibbs*, 1732

fillet
bead

torus

scotia

ovolo

cavetto

cyma recta

cyma reversa

Roman mouldings

Arch of Constantine,
Rome, A.D. 312

10 lower-diameters

Composite Order from James Gibbs (1682-1754), *Rules for Drawing the Several Parts of Architecture*, 1732

RENAISSANCE-BAROQUE

Sources of Italian architectural theory:
1. The study of Roman buildings.
2. The Platonic-Aristotelian description of God and the Universe as a perfect circle.
3. The Pythagorean, and Medieval, idea of Man as the microcosm of the Universe (the macrocosm). 4. The linking of Geometry and Music, two of the Seven Liberal Arts: 'Geometry makes visible the musical consonances' (Boethius, *De Musica*, c.500). In Florence Cosimo de Medici (1389-1462) founded the Platonic Academy.

The Timaeus Plato 427-347 B.C. gives an account of the creation and geometrical form of the universe. He represents the four basic elements and the cosmos as:

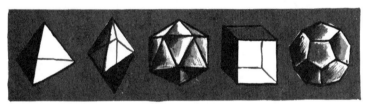

these 'Platonic' bodies are the 5 regular solids. The elements of the cosmos, as well as its soul-substance & its motion, were created proportionate to musical ratios based on Pythagoras (582-c.507 B.C.) He 'regarded numbers as the elements of all things and the whole heaven as a numerical scale' (Aristotle), & found that tones could be measured by striking cords proportionate in length.

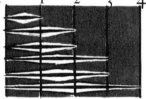

1:2 octave
2:3 fifth
3:4 fourth

Plato gives the 'Harmonic' scale as:

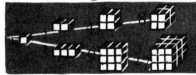

which contain the musical consonances 1:2, 2:3, 3:4.

For Renaissance architect-theorists, churches based upon these axioms, would be microcosms of the universe of God: '. . . the little temples we make ought to resemble this very great one' (Palladio).

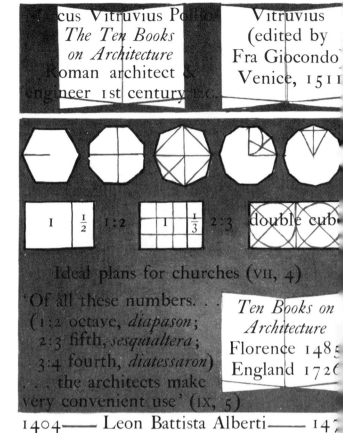

Marcus Vitruvius Pollio *The Ten Books on Architecture* Roman architect & engineer 1st century B.C.

Vitruvius (edited by Fra Giocondo Venice, 1511

Ideal plans for churches (VII, 4) 'Of all these numbers. . . (1:2 octave, *diapason*; 2:3 fifth, *sesquialtera*; 3:4 fourth, *diatessaron*) . . . the architects make very convenient use' (IX, 5)

Ten Books on Architecture Florence 1485 England 1726

1404—— Leon Battista Alberti ——147
Florentine architect and theorist

'the most perfect' 'composite'

Treatise on Architecture civil and milita written c.148

1439—— Francesco di Giorgio ——15
Sienese sculptor and architect

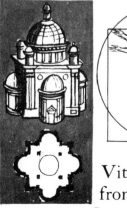

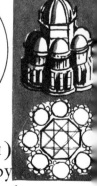

Based on Vitruvius (III, 1) from drawings by

1452—— Leonardo da Vinci ——15

THE DIVINE PROPORTIONS

Vitruvius (edited by Cesarino), Como, 1521	Vitruvius (edited by Barbaro, illustrated by Palladio), Venice, 1556	...chitecture de Vitr... ...u Art de bien bât... mis en français Jean Martin 1546	Vitruvius First English translation 1692

Plans from the fifth book 1547

Seven Books on Architecture 1537-1575

475——— Sebastiano Serlio ———1554
orn Bologna. Architect, worked in France

The Five Orders of Architecture 1562

S. Andrea Rome, 1550

07 — Giacomo Barazzo Da Vignola — 1573

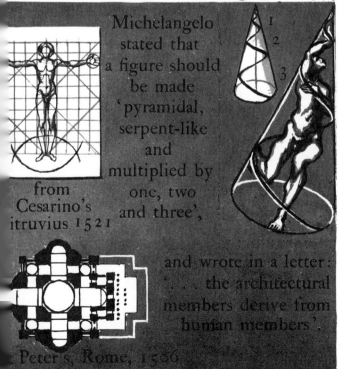

Michelangelo stated that a figure should be made 'pyramidal, serpent-like and multiplied by one, two and three',

from Cesarino's Vitruvius 1521

and wrote in a letter: '.... the architectural members derive from human members'.

Peter's, Rome, 1556

75——— Michelangelo ———1564

08 — Andrea Palladio (pp. 128-9)— 1580

In Baroque churches musical ratios were resolved into an orchestration of visual forces comparable to the fugue, & measured by the eye and the mind of the beholder

S. Andrea al Quirinale, Rome, 1658-7...

1598— Giovanni Lorenzo Bernini —1680
sculptor and architect

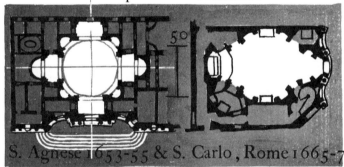

S. Agnese 1653-55 & S. Carlo, Rome 1665-7

1599——— Francesco Borromini ———1667

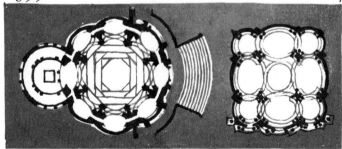

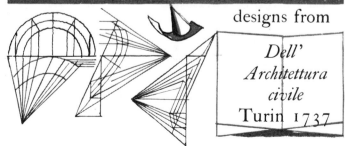

designs from

Dell' Architettura civile Turin 1737

1624——— Guarino Guarini ———1683
mathematician & architect, mostly at Turin

RENAISSANCE – BAROQUE

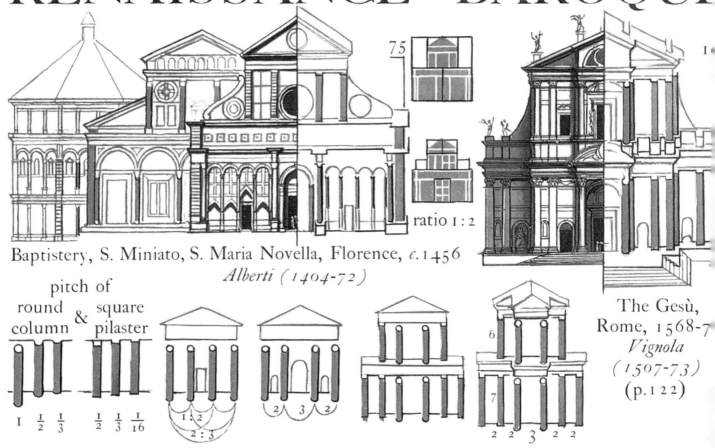

75

ratio 1 : 2

Baptistery, S. Miniato, S. Maria Novella, Florence, *c.*1456
Alberti (1404-72)

The Gesù,
Rome, 1568-7
Vignola
(1507-73)
(p.122)

pitch of
round & square
column pilaster

I   ½   ⅓   ½   ⅓   1/16
      1:2
      2:3
      2 3 2
6
7
2 2 3 2 2

Arrangement & permutations of columns & pilasters to compose a visual 'overture'

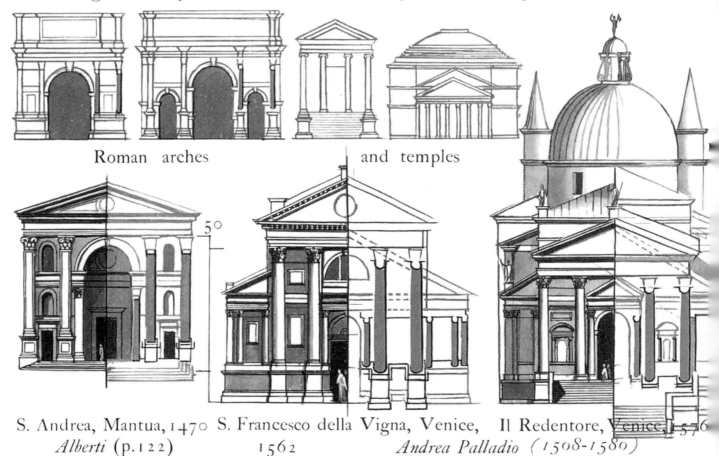

Roman   arches   and   temples

5°

S. Andrea, Mantua, 1470   S. Francesco della Vigna, Venice,   Il Redentore, Venice, 1576
Alberti (p.122)   1562   *Andrea Palladio (1508-1580)*

SS. Martina e Luca,
Rome, 1635-50
Pietro da Cortona
(1596-1669)

S. Agnese in Piazza Navona,
Rome, 1653-55
Francesco Borromini (1599-1667)

S. Maria della Pace,
Rome, 1656-57
Pietro da Cortona
(1596-1669)

S. Susanna, Rome, 1597-1603
Carlo Maderna (1556-1629)

S. Carlo, Rome, 1665-7
Borromini (p.123)

S. Gregorio, Messina, 1660
Guarini (1624-1683)

RENAISSANCE - BAROQUE

entablature block

Romanesque practice of arches supported on columns

100

S. Spirito, Florence, 1435
Filippo Brunelleschi (1377-1446)

Roman practice of carrying arches on square piers

2:3   100

S. Andrea, Mantua, 1472-1512
Alberti (1404-72) (Façade p.120)

The Gesù, Rome, 1568-75
Vignola (1507-73) (Façade p.12
Prototype of Jesuit Baroque church

conchoid
curve *c.*1641

. Carlo alle Quattro Fontane,
Rome, 1638-41
(Façade 1662-67, p.121)
Borromini (1599-1667)

second
project

5°

5°

Architettura Civile

catenary
curve

S. Lorenzo, Turin, 1668-87 *Guarini (1624-83)*

123

The Pantheon,
Rome, A.D. 120-124

142' 6"

St Peter's, Rome
1506-1625
(pp. 91, 116)

137' 6"

138' 6"

Florence
Cathedral:
Dome, 1420-34
Brunelleschi
(1377-1446)
(pp. 91, 109, 116)

Circular temples,
Vitruvius (IV, 9)

30

100

c

c

c

c. chains

Tempietto, S. Pietro in
Montorio, Rome, 1502-10
Bramante (1444-1514)

Dome 1564-9
Michelangelo
(1475-1564)

S. Ivo della Sapienza,
Rome, 1642-50,
Borromini
(1599-1667)

50

St Paul's
Cathedral,
London,
1675-1710
Wren (1631-1723)
(pp. 146-7)

100

101

The Dome of the
Invalides, Paris,
1693-1706 *Jules*
Hardouin-Mansart
(1646-1708)
(p.131)

100

Sanctuary, Vallinotto, near Turin, 1738-9
Bernard   Vittone (1704/5-70)

RENAISSANCE - BAROQUE

rusticated
masonry
after
Serlio

Palazzo del Tè, Mantua, 1526-3
Giulio Romano (1492-1546)

Doric Ionic Corinthian

Palazzo Medici-Riccardi, Florence, 1430
Michelozzo (1397-1473)

Palazzo Rucellai, Cancelleria, Rome, House of Raphael, Palazzo Thiene, Vicenza, 1556-
Florence, 1451 1495-1505 Rome *c.*1512 *Andrea Palladio (1508-1580,*
Alberti (1404-72) *Bramante (1444-1514)*

The Capitol, Rome, 1540-1644, *Michelangelo (1475-1564)* The 'Colossal' Orde

ITALY, PALACES

cycloidal curves
Pascal (1623-1662)

Collegio Propaganda
Fide, Rome 1646-66
Borromini (1599-1667)

Palazzo Carignano,
Turin, *c*.1678-80
Guarini (1624-1683)

Palazzo Farnese, Caprarola, 1559-1564 *Giacomo Barozzi da Vignola (1507-1573)*

127

RENAISSANCE - BAROQUE

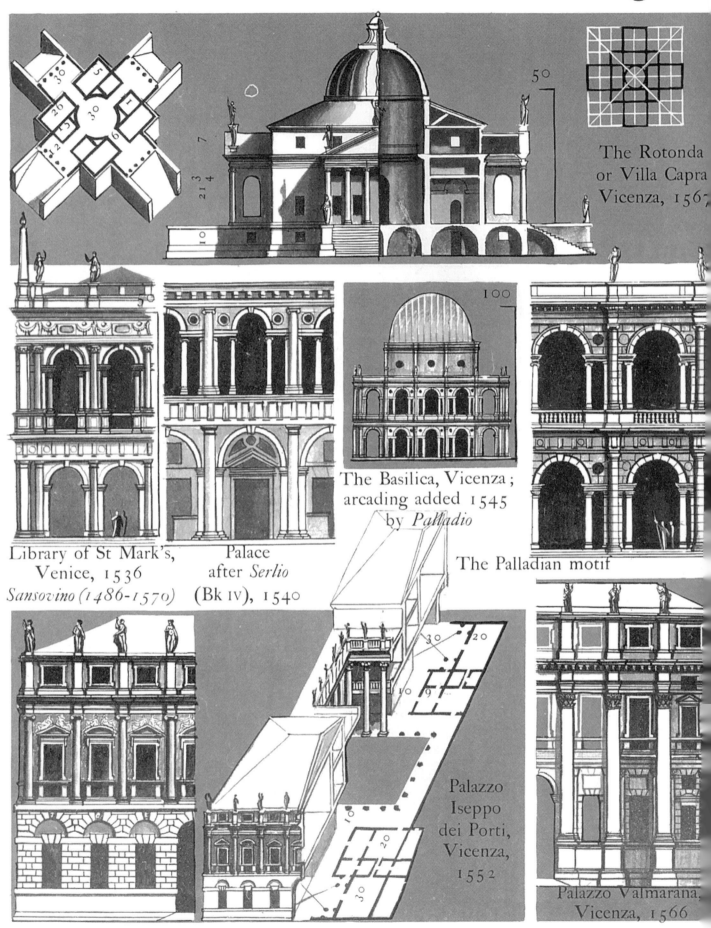

The Rotonda
or Villa Capra
Vicenza, 1567

The Basilica, Vicenza;
arcading added 1545
by *Palladio*

The Palladian motif

Library of St Mark's,
Venice, 1536
Sansovino (1486-1570)

Palace
after *Serlio*
(Bk IV), 1540

Palazzo
Iseppo
dei Porti,
Vicenza,
1552

Palazzo Valmarana,
Vicenza, 1566

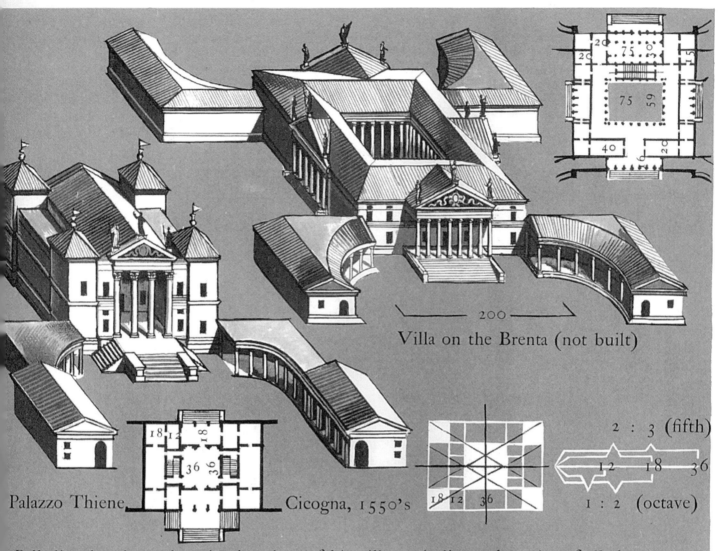

Villa on the Brenta (not built)

Palazzo Thiene

Cicogna, 1550's

2 : 3 (fifth)

1 : 2 (octave)

Palladio placed numbers in the plans of his villas to indicate the ratios of all the rooms in the building; these often followed the ratios given by Vitruvius and Alberti

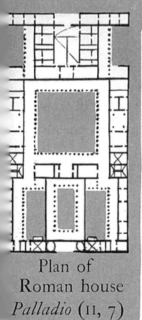

Plan of
Roman house
Palladio (II, 7)

Andrea Palladio (1508-1580)

designed many buildings in and around his native Vicenza, mostly of brick faced with stucco. He studied classical architecture in Rome 1545-47. His treatise

I Quattro Libri dell' Architettura, Venice, 1570

influenced the design of buildings in Europe, especially in England

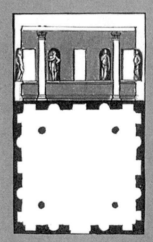

Hall of four columns
or Roman tetrastyle
Palladio (II, 8)

(p.117)

after *Serlio*
1537

25

50

St Gervais, Paris:
façade, 1616
Salomon de Brosse
(c.1562-1626)

50

Château d'Anet: chapel, 1549-53
Philibert de l'Orme (c.1510-1570)

Church of the Sorbonne, Paris, *c.1635*
Jacques Lemercier (c.1580/5-1654)

The Italian campaigns of the French Kings, Charles VIII (1483-98),
Louis XII (1498-1515) and Francis I (1515-47), failed in their aims;
instead France was invaded by the ideas and the arts of the Italian Renaissance.

FRANCE, CHURCHES

(pp. 56, 117)

(p. 124)

Church of
the Invalides,
Paris, 1680-91
*Jules
Hardouin
Mansart
(1646-1708)*

Panthéon
(St Généviève),
Paris, 1764-90
*Jacques-
Germain
Soufflot
(1713-80)*

Château
de Chambord,
1519-1547

Leonardo da Vinci

2 00

9 0

Château de Maisons,
1642-46
François Mansart
(1598-1666)

1 00

B.   1600-09   *Jacques du Cerceau*
(c.1550-1614)
Palais des Tuileries,   (Remodelled
1564-1680   1860-65)
(Destroyed 1871)

5 0

A   B   C   D

500

River Seine

1 0

5 0

A.   Central pavilion, 1570-1592
Philibert de l'Orme (c.1515-1570)

Palais du Louvre,
Paris, 1546-1878

C.   Course du Vie
Louvre,   begun 15
Pierre Lescot (c.1510-7

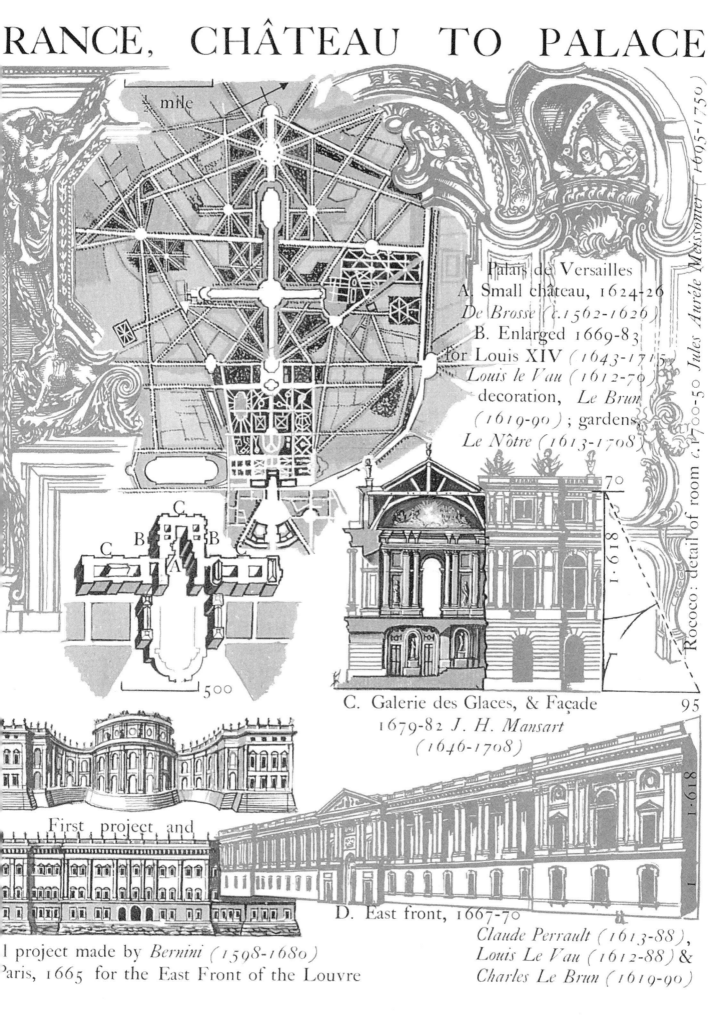

mile

Palais de Versailles
A. Small château, 1624-26
De Brosse (c.1562-1626)
B. Enlarged 1669-83
for Louis XIV (1643-1715)
Louis le Vau (1612-70)
decoration, Le Brun
(1619-90); gardens,
Le Nôtre (1613-1708)

Rococo: detail of room c.1700-50 Jules Aurèle Meissonier (1695-1750)

C B B
C A C

500

70

1.618

C. Galerie des Glaces, & Façade
1679-82 J. H. Mansart
(1646-1708)

95

1.618

First project and

D. East front, 1667-70

l project made by Bernini (1598-1680)
aris, 1665 for the East Front of the Louvre

Claude Perrault (1613-88),
Louis Le Vau (1612-88) &
Charles Le Brun (1619-90)

RENAISSANCE-BAROQUE

Gable of a house, Heidelburg, c.1600

The Castle, Heidelburg, 1531-1612; the Heinrichsbau, 1556-63

200

main entrance   staircase in east wing

Palace, Berlin, 1698-1706

Andreas Schluter (c.1664-1714)

Palace Schwarzenberg, Vienna, 1706-1725

Johann Berhard Fischer von Erla (1656-1723)

A

The Zwinger, Dresden, 1711-1722:
the palace forecourt
Mathaeus Daniel Pöpplemann (1662-1736)

A. Gate pavilion

5°

Episcopal palace, Bruchsal, 1730: staircase

Johann Balthasar Neumann (1687-1753)

The Gesù, Rome, 1668-83 (p.122): fresco and stucco figures on nave vault, 1674-79, 'Adoration of the Name of Jesus'
Giovanni Battista Gaulli (1639-1709)

S. Andrea in Valle, Rome, 1591-1623: fresco in dome, 'The Virgin in Glory'
Giovanni Lanfranco (1582-1647)

orbital path of observer

Italian Baroque churches

Vaults, domes and apses were frequently 'opened out' to heaven by means of *sotto in sù* (Italian: 'from below upwards'), illusionist paintings, and often reinforced by three-dimensional figures

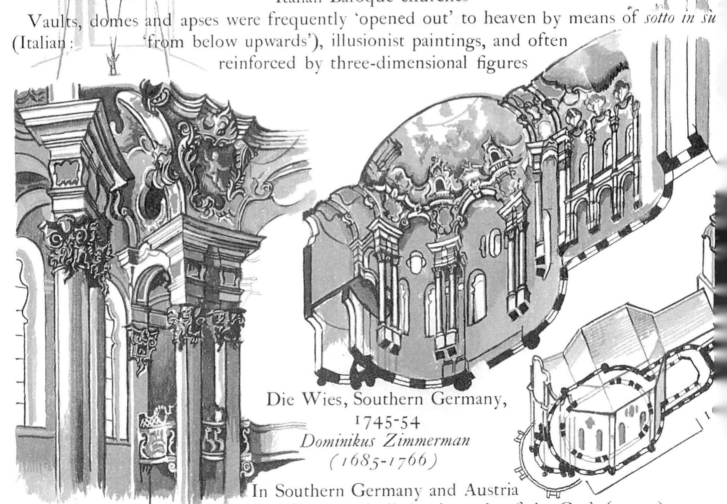

Die Wies, Southern Germany, 1745-54
Dominikus Zimmerman
(1685-1766)

In Southern Germany and Austria many Jesuit Baroque churches were built in the style of the Gesù (p.122). The Thirty Years' War (1618-48) was followed by a resurgence of church-building in which all the arts—architecture, sculpture, painting and music—were fused into Roco-

Vierzehnheiligen, Southern Germany,
1744-7²
Balthasar Neumann (1687-1753),
rchitect, mathematican, military engineer, town-planner,
designer of fountains, bell-caster; possessed Guarini's
'Architettura Civile, 1737 (p.123)

jets of water describe parabolic curves

ele

pse

hyperbola

parabola

parabolic, forward tilted, three-dimensional arches

RENAISSANCE-BAROQUE

I 'Plateresque'(*platero* = silversmith), from the use of extravagant decoration 1492-1556

3

9

$3\frac{1}{2}$

$2\frac{1}{2}$

200

A

Portal of Pardon,
1536 *Siloé*

Cathedral, Granada,
'designed in the Roman
to the conquest of the
Diego de Siloé

begun 1528 and
manner' as a memorial
Spanish Moors in 1492
(c.1495-1563)

II Herreran style or '*Estilo desornamentado*' (plain style), 1556-1650: adaptation of th
design of the Italian High Renaissance by *Juan de Herrera* *(c.1530-97)*

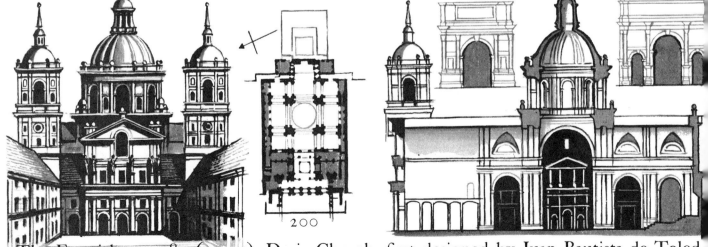

200

The Escorial 1574-82 (p.115), Doric Church, first designed by Juan Bautista de Toled
(d.1567), philosopher and mathematician, who worked under Michelangelo;
redesigned by *Juan de Herrera (c.1530-97)* built in yellow-grey granite, in 2:3 ratio

III   'Churrigueresque',   named after *José de   Churriguera*
(*1665-1723*)

Cathedral,
Santiago
de Compostella:

west façade,
known as
'El Obradoiro',
*c.*1738
*Fernando
de Casas y Novoa*
(*fl. 1711-94*)

Charterhouse sacristy, Granada, 1713-47.
Designed by *Francisco Hurtado* (*1669-1725*), begun 1730
by *Luis de Arévalo* (*1727-64*), stonemason; plasterwork by *Luis Cabello*

RENAISSANCE - BAROQUE

Treatises on
Architecture known in
Elizabethan England:

ITALIAN

Vitruvius
Alberti, 1485
Vignola, 1562
Serlio, 1537-75
(pp.118-119)
Palladio, 1570
(p.129)

FRENCH

Philibert de l'Orme
(*c*.1510-1570)
Nouvelles Inventions
Paris, 1561
Architecture Paris,1568

J. A. du Cerceau
(*c*.1510-85)
Architecture, 1559
*Les Plus Excellents
Bâtiments de France*,
1576-1579

GERMAN & FLEMISH

Hans Blum
*Quinque Columnarum,
etc.* Zurich, 1550

Vreedman de Vries
(1527-1604)
Architectura
Antwerp, 1563
Compartimenta
Antwerp, 1566

Wendel Dietterlin
(*c*.1550-1599)
Architectura
Nuremberg, 1594-98

Hampton Court Palace

c.1525

Serlio
1545

Somerset House, London
(demolished *c*.1777)

1547-52

John Shute
(d.1563)
*The First and
Chief Groundes
of Architecture*
London, 1563

THVSCANA   IONICA   COMPOSITA, OR ITALIC

Dietterlin

Charlton House, Greenwich

c.1610

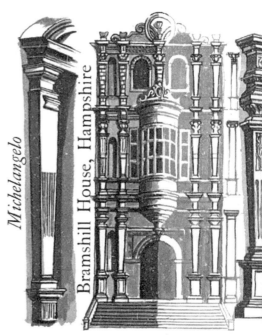

Michelangelo

Bramshill House, Hampshire

1605-12

...ge, Cambridge

1572-73

Raynham, Norfolk

c.1635

Amesbury, Wilts: original façade *John Webb (1611-72)*

1661

Blenheim Palace, Oxfordshire
Sir John Vanbrugh

1705-24

Hardwick Hall, Derbyshire, 1590-97
*Probably by Robert Smythson
(c.1536-1614)*

Queen's House, Greenwich, 1616-35
Inigo Jones

5°

Easton Neston, Northants, 1669-c.1712
N. Hawksmoor

Mereworth Castle, Kent, 1723
Colen Campbell

Burghley House, Northamptonshire

c.1550

1577-83

Arch of Constantine, Rome

James Gibbs
(1682-1754)
The Rules for Drawing the Several Parts of Architecture,
London, 1732

Tuscan   *Dorick*   *Ionick*   *Corinthian*

RENAISSANCE-BAROQUE

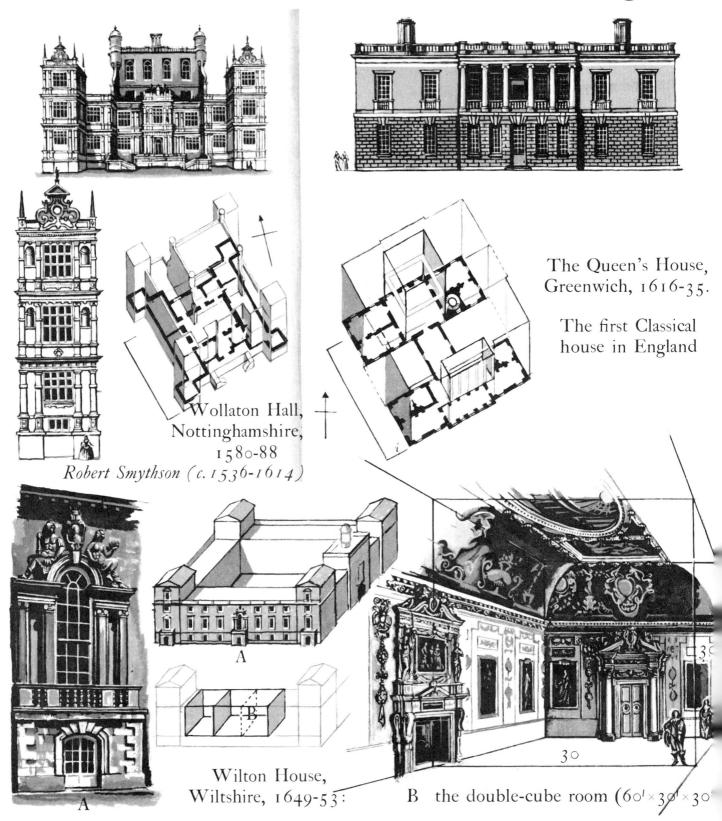

The Queen's House,
Greenwich, 1616-35.

The first Classical
house in England

Wollaton Hall,
Nottinghamshire,
1580-88

Robert Smythson (c. 1536-1614)

A

B

Wilton House,
Wiltshire, 1649-53:

B the double-cube room (60' × 30' × 30')

Inigo Jones (1573-1642) 'picture-maker' and architect; visited Italy *c.* 1601-03;
designed court-masques, often collaborating with Ben Jonson until 1631.
Visited Italy again 1613-14; annotated a copy of Palladio's *Architecture*.

double
cube

110

55

75' 6"

Pal. Barbarano, Vicenza,
Palladio

The Banqueting Hall, Whitehall, 1619-22

reliminary designs for the Banqueting Hall

Project for Whitehall Palace
John Webb (1611-72)
assistant to
Inigo Jones

1280

Tuscan temple
Vitruvius (IV, 7)
(p.58)

5²

3⁰

110⁴

Old St Paul's: west front, begun 1633
(burnt down 1666)

St Paul's Church, 1631 & Covent Garden Piazza, London, begun 1630
(rebuilt 1795)   (later demolished)

RENAISSANCE - BAROQUE

Pre-Fire Design for
a domed crossing,
'in a Latine style'
1666

Old St Paul's,
destroyed in
the Great Fire, 1666

The Pantheon Design
c. 1668-69

Basilica of Constantine
Palladio

Centralized designs 'after a Roman manner',
remote from 'the Gothick rudeness
of ye old Design'.
The chapter
'thought the model not
enough of a cathedral fashion',
and a longitudinal plan,
based on the Latin Cross,
was adopted.

Greek Cross Design, c. 1672

The Great
Model, 1673

elevations

plans

The Warrant Design, before 1675

Projects for St Paul's Cathedral, London, by *Sir Christopher Wren*

ENGLAND, WREN & THE BAROQUE

outer dome of timber
covered with
sheet lead,
on a brick cone
18" thick,
also
with an inner
brick dome
18" thick

355' 6"

C chains

Study
for
dome

St Peter's, Rome:
dome *Bramante*
(1444-1514)
(from Serlio)

The
mathematician
Robert Hooke
wrote that
Wren used the
'catenary line'

St Paul's Cathedral, London,
*c.*1675-1711
Sir Christopher Wren
(1631-1723)
Vaulting of brick,
walls of ashlar stone
with rubble filling,
façades of Portland stone

100

100

100

Section
of nave

145

RENAISSANCE - BAROQUE

Sir Christopher Wren (1632-1723).

Early scientific pursuits: optics, hyperbolic
lenses & a treatise on cycloids.
Newton in the *Principia* described Wren
as 'one of the greatest geometers
of our times'.
Professor of Astronomy, London 1657
and Oxford 1661.
First architectural works 1662.
Studied buildings in and around
Paris 1665; met F. Mansart,
Le Vau, Bernini and
probably Guarini.

226' 11"

215' 1"

100

50

50

50

100

St Bride, Fleet Street,
1670-84; spire, 1701-3

St Mary-le-Bow,
Cheapside, 1670-83

The fire of London lasted from -5 September 1666. On 1 September

Wren submitted a plan for rebuilding the City of London.

St Paul's

½ mile

hough this plan was later abandoned, of the 87 churches destroyed 52 were redesigned by Wren as preaching halls for Protestant services.

80

50

50

50

50

St James, Garlickhythe 1674-87

St Mary, Abchurch, 1681-86

50

St Mary-at-Hill, 1670-76

St Stephen, Walbrook, 1672-77

St Antholin, 1682 (Demolished 1874)

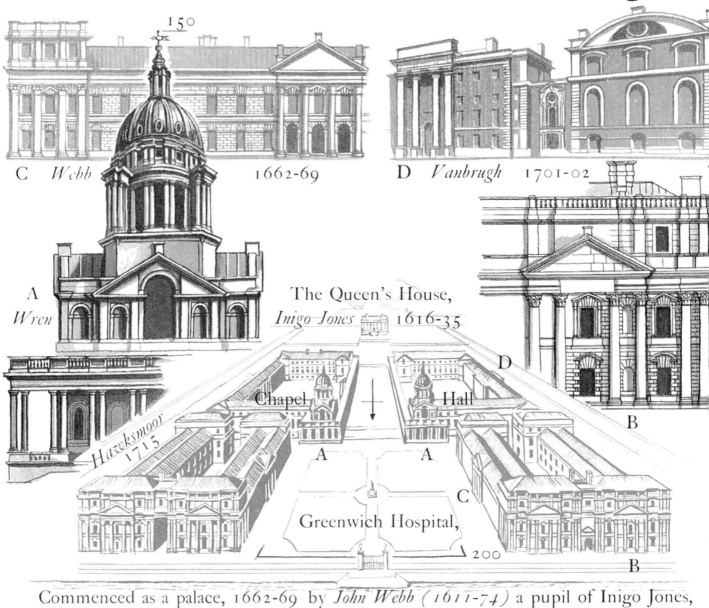

150

C *Webb* 1662-69

D *Vanbrugh* 1701-02

A *Wren*

Hawksmoor 1715

The Queen's House,
Inigo Jones 1616-35

Chapel

Hall

D

B

A A

C

Greenwich Hospital,

200

B

Commenced as a palace, 1662-69 by *John Webb (1611-74)* a pupil of Inigo Jones,
was incorporated into an extensive scheme for a Hospital by *Wren*

*wings
18th
century*

Goose Pie House, Whitehall:
Vanbrugh's House, *c.*1700

Vanbrugh's House, Esher, 1711
'the embattled manner'

Vanbrugh Castle,
Greenwich, *c.*1717

Sir John Vanbrugh (1664-1726) commissioned in the army; playwright 1696-1705;
became an architect 1699.   Hawksmoor worked with Vanbrugh on his four great hous

ENGLISH BAROQUE

A

B

salon
hall
A

B
gate
pavilion
kitchen
court

kitchen
court

great   court

stable
court

150

enheim Palace,
Oxfordshire
1705-24
Vanbrugh

table
ourt

great

100

kitchen
court

court

Seaton
Delaval,
Northumber-
land,
1720-29
Vanbrugh

RENAISSANCE · BAROQUE

Tomb of Metella, Rome, *c.* 10 B.C.: engraving by *Bartoli* 1697, used by *Hawksmoor* for the Mausoleum, Castle Howard

65

the Mausoleum, Castle Howard, Yorkshire, begun 1729

Reconstruction of the Mausoleum, Halicarnassus, 353 B.C. ascribed to *Hawksmoor*

100

St Anne, Limehouse, London, 1712-24
Hawksmoor

St George, Bloomsbury, London, 1720-30

St Mary Woolnoth, 1716-2[

Nicholas Hawksmoor (1661-1736)
clerk and assistant to Wren, worked with Vanbrugh until the latter's death in 1726.
Built six London churches under the Act for 'Building… fifty new churches', 1711,
had schemes for replanning Oxford and Cambridge in a Roman manner

The
Ratcliffe
Camera,
Oxford,
1739-49
Gibbs

Drawing for the Ratcliffe
Camera, Oxford, by
Hawksmoor, *c.*1714

100

100

St Martin-in-the-Fields, London, 1721-26

James Gibbs
(1682-1754)
St Paul,   *A Book of*   Travelled in   *Rules for*
Deptford,   *Architecture*   Holland,   *Drawing the*
London,   London   France & Italy   *Several Parts*
1730   1728   1694-1709   *of*
Thomas Archer   & worked under   *Architecture*
(1668-1743)   *Carlo Fontana*   London
Travelled in Italy   *(1634-1714)*   1732
c. 1689-93   in Rome 1707-09

50

Burlington House, London, *c*.1717

Colen Campbell

Wanstead House, Essex, 1715-20 (demolished 182

Villa Rotonda
Palladio

Mereworth
Castle,
Kent,
1723

*Colen
Campbell*

Chiswick
House,
London,
begun
1725

Lord Burlington

Design b
Palladio (
Scammozz
(1552-161

Palladio (pp.128-9)		Colen Campbell (d.1729)	William Kent (1685-1748)	Lord Burlingt (1694-1753)
I Quattro Libri dell' Architettura Venice 1570	translated by Nicholas Dubois 1715-17, with plates by Giacomo Leoni	*Vitruvius Britannicus* 1715-17 100 engravings of classical houses in England. Praised both Palladio and Inigo Jones	*Designs of Inigo Jones* 1727	*Fabbriche antiche* 1730 engravings fro Palladio's drawi

Increase of trade & agricultural prosperity enriched the nobility,
who built country houses which, in reaction to the Baroque, followed the classical rules
the Augustan Age, *c*.1680-1750. *Lord Burlington (1694-1753)* went on the Grand To
to Italy in 1714-15 and 1719 to study Palladio's buildings, and, with *Colen Campbell,*
William Kent, Giacomo Leoni and others, developed the Palladian style in England

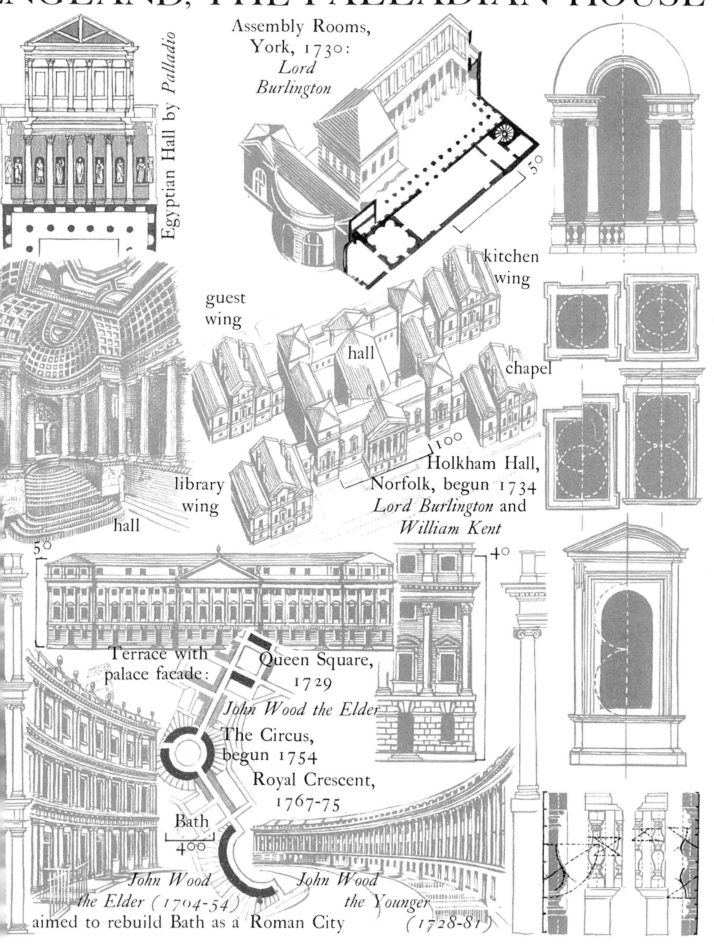

Egyptian Hall by *Palladio*

Assembly Rooms, York, 1730: *Lord Burlington*

5°

kitchen wing

guest wing

hall

chapel

library wing

hall

Holkham Hall, Norfolk, begun 1734 *Lord Burlington* and *William Kent*

100

5°

4°

Terrace with palace facade:

Queen Square, 1729

John Wood the Elder

The Circus, begun 1754

Royal Crescent, 1767-75

Bath

400

John Wood the Elder (1704-54) aimed to rebuild Bath as a Roman City

John Wood the Younger (1728-81)

RENAISSANCE - BAROQUE

Prior Park, Bath, 1735-43:
John Wood the Elder (1704-54)

Palladian bridge, 1756

Revival of Greek
architecture *c.*1750

James Stuart (1713-88)
& Nicholas Revett
(*c.*1721-1804)
*The Antiquities
of Athens*
1762

The Parthenon
The Antiquities of Athens

From *c.*1700
onwards,
the Grand Tour
was made
through the
Alps into Italy,
and the

'beautiful'

prospects
of Claude,
and the

'sublime'

landscapes
of Rosa
were brought
back to England

Claude Lorraine (1600-82)

Salvator Rosa (1615-73)

*Giovanni Battista
Piranesi
(1720-78)*
Italian artist,
published etchings
of Roman
magnificence,
antique & Baroque,
& prison interiors,
which exerted
a great influence
on architecture
in Europe.

Belvedere, Claremont,
Surrey, 1715 *Vanbrugh*

All Souls College, Oxford,
*c.*1730 *Hawksmoor*

Landscape *Robert Adam (1728-9*

ENGLAND, THE PICTURESQUE

The High School, Edinburgh, begun 1825 *Thomas Hamilton* *(1785-1858)*

St Pancras, London, 1818-22 *H. W. Inwood (1794-1843)*

Somerset House, London: ...ver front, 1776-86 *Sir William Chambers (1723-96)*

Rotunda, Bank of England, London, 1788-1808 *Sir John Soane (1753-1837)*

...ewgate Prison, London, begun 1769 (demolished 1902) *...eorge Dance II (1741-1825)*

...awberry Hill, Twickenham, begun ...748 *Horace Walpole (1717-97)*

Fonthill Abbey, Wiltshire, 1795-1807 *James Wyatt (1747-1813)*

RENAISSANCE - BAROQUE

Fontana
Trevi,
Rome,
1732-1762
Salvi

Kedleston Hall

100

33' 6"

50

Kedleston Hall, Derbyshire, 1756-70
designed by *James Paine (1725-89)*;
south front & interior by
Robert Adam (1728-92).
Studied in Italy 1754-58

26, Grosvenor Square, London,
1773-74 *Adam* (demolished 186

Pitzhanger Place, Middlesex,
1800-1803

Bank Stock Office, Bank of Englar
1792-93 (demolished 1927)

Sir John Soane (1753-1837) Visited Italy 1778-1780

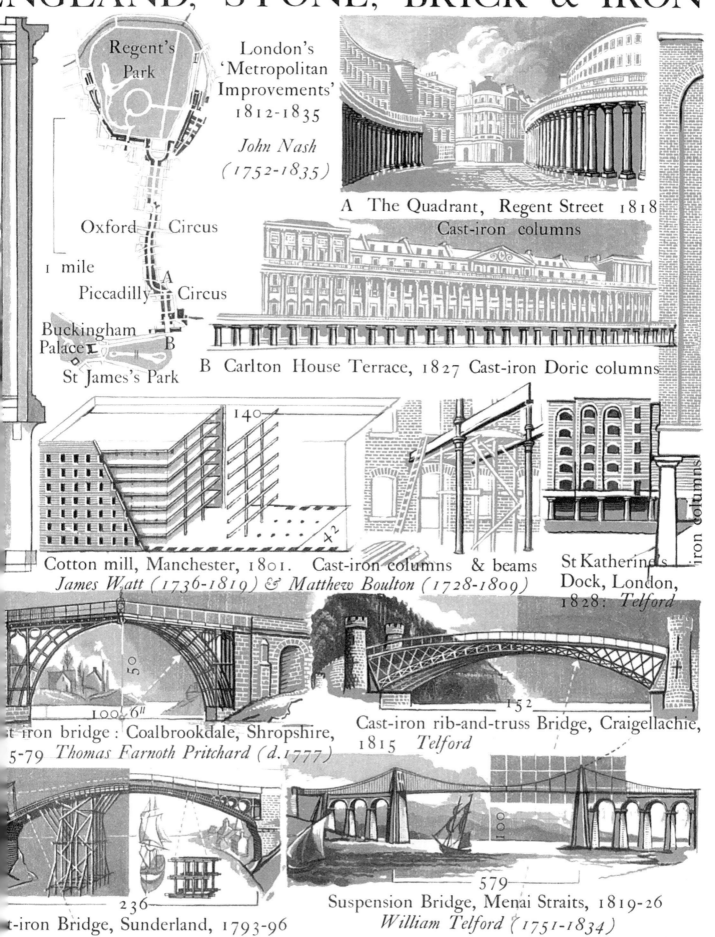

Regent's Park

London's 'Metropolitan Improvements' 1812-1835

John Nash (1752-1835)

Oxford Circus

1 mile

Piccadilly Circus

Buckingham Palace

St James's Park

A   The Quadrant, Regent Street   1818
Cast-iron columns

B   Carlton House Terrace, 1827 Cast-iron Doric columns

140

42

Cotton mill, Manchester, 1801.   Cast-iron columns & beams
James Watt (1736-1819) & Matthew Boulton (1728-1809)

St Katherine's Dock, London, 1828: *Telford*

Iron columns

50

100 6"

Cast iron bridge : Coalbrookdale, Shropshire,
5-79 *Thomas Farnoth Pritchard (d.1777)*

152

Cast-iron rib-and-truss Bridge, Craigellachie,
1815   *Telford*

100

236

Cast-iron Bridge, Sunderland, 1793-96

579

Suspension Bridge, Menai Straits, 1819-26
William Telford (1751-1834)

A.D.   1000   1500   1700   1800   1850   19

Columbus

1492

Magellan 1497-9

Russia

U.S.A.

Spanish
1763

Portuguese   English
Trade and Colonies

100

Roman   Renaissance

Greek   Gothic   Baroque

photography
1839

glider

printing
c.1459

steam
engine
1769

petrol
engine   1873

c.1750   INDUSTRIAL REVOLUTION

Copernicus
(1473-1543)

Newton
(1642-1727)

Gauss
(1777-
1855)

Faraday
(1791-
1867)
first
dynamo
1834

Clerk
Maxwell
(1831-
1879)
electro-
magnetism
1864

constant
speed
of light
18,600
miles
per
second

Mar
Curi
(186
193.
radi
activ
radi

earth

sun

a

b   c

abc > 180°

curved
space

1887

The
Roman
Empire

The
Medieval
Universe

1543

law of gravitation
1687

1792 - 1865

Capitol, Washington   Houses of Parliament,
London
1840-65

Eifel Tower

Parthenon, Athens

Pantheon, Rome

Beauvais Cathedral

St Peter's, Rome

St Paul's, London

579

Menai suspension bridge, 1819-21

buildings in black to the same scale

100   500

Crystal Palace, London, 1851

timber   stone   brick   cast iron   wrought iron   steel (mass-produc

Portland cement   reinforced concr

INTRODUCTION

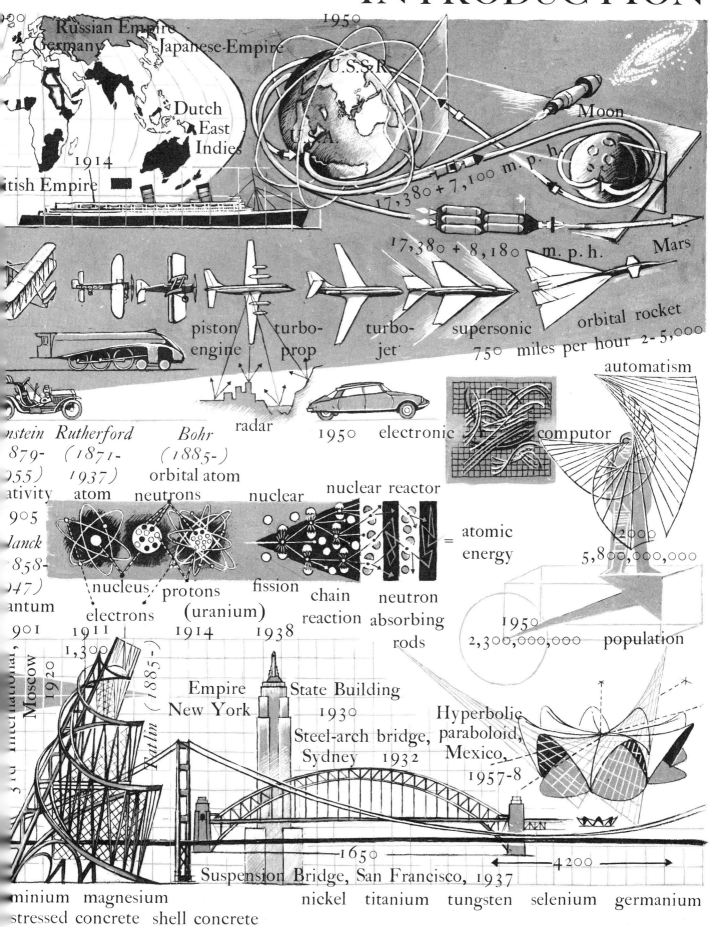

Russian Empire
Germany — Japanese Empire

U.S.S.R.

Dutch East Indies

1914

Moon

British Empire

17,380 + 7,100 m. p. h.

17,380 + 8,180 m. p. h. Mars

piston engine turbo-prop turbo-jet supersonic orbital rocket

750 miles per hour 2-5,000

automatism

radar 1950 electronic computor

Einstein Rutherford Bohr
(1879- (1871- (1885-)
1955) 1937) orbital atom

relativity atom neutrons nuclear nuclear reactor

1905

Planck
(1858-
1947)

quantum

1901

nucleus protons fission chain neutron
electrons (uranium) reaction absorbing
1911 1914 1938 rods

atomic energy

2000
5,800,000,000

1950
2,300,000,000 population

3rd International,
Moscow 1920

1,300

Tatlin (1885-)

Empire
New York

State Building
1930

Steel-arch bridge,
Sydney 1932

Hyperbolic
paraboloid,
Mexico,
1957-8

1650

4200

Suspension Bridge, San Francisco, 1937

aluminium magnesium nickel titanium tungsten selenium germanium
stressed concrete shell concrete

19TH & 20TH CENTURIES

22 churches and chapels built by
*Augustus Welby Northmore Pugin
(1812-52)*
from frontispiece to
*An Apology for the
Revival of
Christian Architecture,*
1843

The Houses of Parliament,
London, 1840-65 *Sir Charles
Barry (1795-1860),*
assisted by *Pugin*
iron
roof

John Ruskin
(1819-1900)
*The Seven Lamps
of Architecture*
1849
*The Stones
of Venice,*
1851

300

cast-iron
dome
*Sidney Smirke
(1799-1877)*

British Museum,
London, 1824-47
*Sir Robert Smirke
(1780-1817)*

Gothic

The Red House, Kent, 18
Philip Webb (1831-191
for *William Morris
(1834-96)*

Regency Villas, Cheltenham,
*c.*1825

Classic

1608

The Crystal Pal
Sydenham, London, 185
Paxton; water towers, *Brunel*
(Moved from Hyde Park, p.163)

Clifton Suspension Bridge, Bristol,
designed 1829-31;

702

begun 1836
Isambard Kingdom Brunel (1806-59)

St Pancras Station, London, 1865-73. Engine
W.H.Barlow (1812-1902) & M.Ordish (1824-
Hotel, 1865-75 *Sir George Gilbert Scott (1810-*

ENGLAND

School of Art, Glasgow, 1896 Art Nouveau *Charles Rennie Mackintosh (1868-1928)*

Projected Roman Catholic Cathedral, Liverpool, *Sir Edwin Lutyens (1869-1944)* 1929-41 succeeded 1962 by the design of *Frederick Gibberd (1908-)*

34°

Village College, Impington, Cambridgeshire, 1936 *Walter Gropius (1883-)* (pp. 174-5) *& Edwin Maxwell Fry (1899-)*

House, Rutland, 1901 *Charles Annesley Voysey (1857-1941)*

3°

House, Sussex, 1937 *F. R. S. Yorke (1906-62) & Marcel Breuer (1902-):* born Hungary, U.S.A. 1937

steel frame

...eal & Son Store, London, ...10-14 *Smith & Brewer*

Peter Jones Store, London, 1936-39 *William Crabtree*

auditorium insulated by foyers

— compression

tension

Royal Festival Hall, London, 1951 *Robert Hogg Matthew (1906-)*

366 360

St Paul's London

1,710

The Forth Bridge, 1882-1890 *Sir Benjamin Baker & Sir John Fowler*

19TH & 20TH CENTURIES

CAST IRON

is the direct result of smelting iron ore in a blast furnace with coke.

valve

air heater

slag molten iron

The liquid ore solidifies on cooling & can be given the desired shape by being poured into moulds. The process was first carried out *c.*1710 by *Benjamin Darby (1677-1717)*. Cast iron is brittle & reacts to bending stress. Used primarily for vertical columns

WROUGHT IRON

is obtained by oxidizing white-hot cast iron. It is puddled (purified) from an excess of carbon & impurities in a 'reverberatory' furnace, introduced by Henry Cort *c.*1760s.

Ductile and malleable, wrought-iron can be pulled out into wire or rolled into beams

STEEL

is made from cast-iron, the carbon being burnt out by a blast of air through the molten metal in a 'Converter',

invented by Sir Henry Bessemer in 1856. Steel has equal strength in compression and tension

Sir William Fairbairn

*c.*1845

Victoria Station London 1861

Cast-iron column,

THE BEAM

compression

tension

flange
web
flange

& TRUSS

compression boom

S.

tension boom

S. compression or strut
T. tension or tie

rivets

bolt

Cast-iron column and wrought-iron beams,

Cast-iron column,

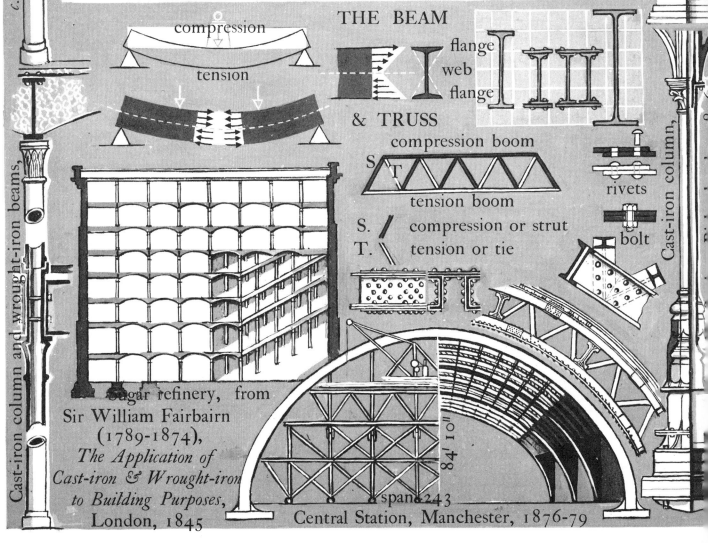

Sugar refinery, from
Sir William Fairbairn
(1789-1874),
*The Application of
Cast-iron & Wrought-iron
to Building Purposes,*
London, 1845

84' 10"

span 243

Central Station, Manchester, 1876-79

162

CAST IRON, WROUGHT IRON, STEEL

Design for wrought-iron column: Viollet-le-Duc (1814-79), from Lectures on Architecture.

The Crystal Palace, Hyde Park, London, 1851 *Sir Joseph Paxton (1803-1865)*

Paris, 1863-72

984

1848

408

Constructed in 17 weeks in cast-iron with pre-fabricated standardized parts and based on multiples of 24 feet standard glass size 49″ by 10″

The Fair Building, Chicago, U.S.A., 1891 *William Le Baron Jenny (1832- 1907)*

Brussels, 1893

Victor Horta (1861-1947)

hinge base

The Eiffel Tower, Paris, 1887-89. Constructed of wrought-iron *Gustave Eiffel (1832-1923)*

to which cross beams form a rigid framework

steel beams are rivetted to

span 375

150 ft

Galerie des Machines, International Exhibition, Paris, 1889: three-hinged steel arch *Dutert*; engineer *Cottamin*

Japanese print

Hokusai (1760-1849)

Casa Battló ('House of the bones'), Barcelona, 1903-07 *Gaudí*

Parc Güell, Barcelona, 1900-14 *Gaudí*

tilted helicoid columns

Wire model of ribs with weights hung proportional to the loads to be carried

Project for Güell Colony chapel, nr Barcelona 1898-1914 *Gaudí*

Antoni Gaudí (1852-1926): born Reus, near Tarragona; worked & died in Barcelona. 'Gau

SPAIN, MODERNISMO, GAUDÍ

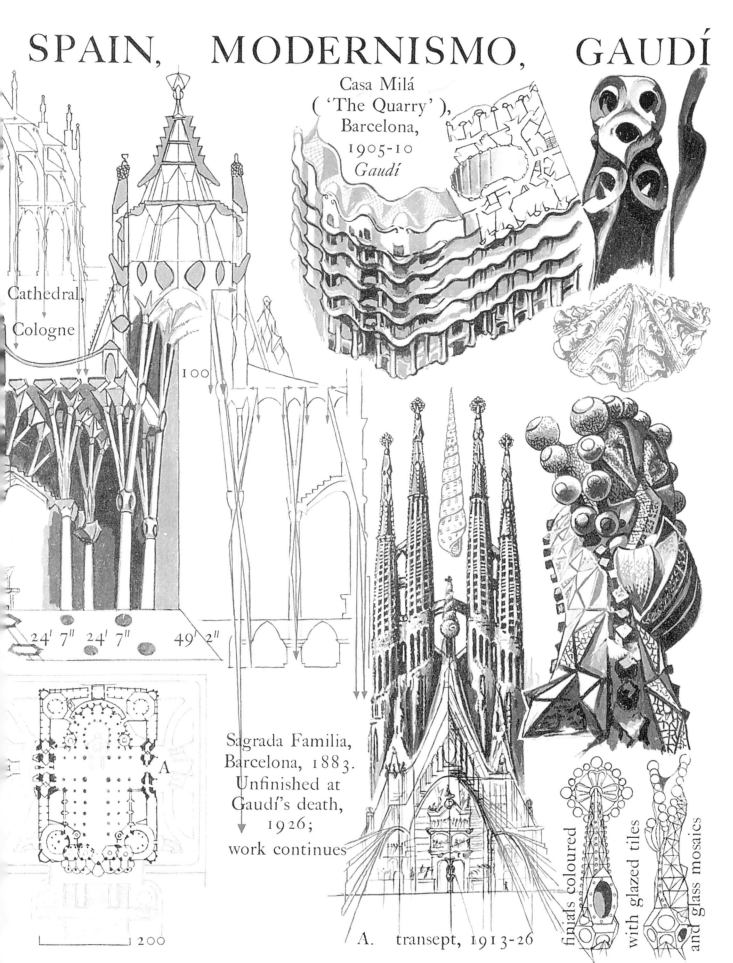

Casa Milá ('The Quarry'), Barcelona, 1905-10 *Gaudí*

Cathedral, Cologne

100

24' 7"   24' 7"   49' 2"

200

Sagrada Familia, Barcelona, 1883. Unfinished at Gaudí's death, 1926; work continues

A.   transept, 1913-26

finials coloured

with glazed tiles

and glass mosaics

the constructor of 1900, the professional builder in stone, iron and brick' *Le Corbusier*

19 TH & 20 TH CENTURIES

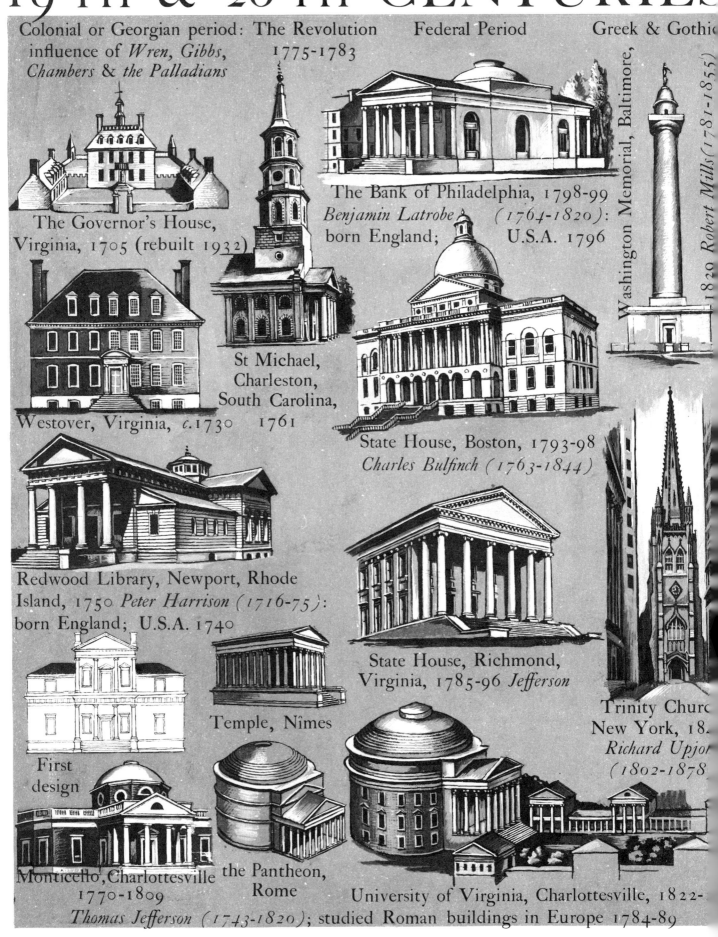

Colonial or Georgian period: The Revolution
influence of *Wren, Gibbs,*
Chambers & the Palladians

1775-1783

Federal Period

Greek & Gothic

The Governor's House,
Virginia, 1705 (rebuilt 1932)

St Michael,
Charleston,
South Carolina,
1761

The Bank of Philadelphia, 1798-99
Benjamin Latrobe *(1764-1820):*
born England; U.S.A. 1796

Washington Memorial, Baltimore,
1820 Robert Mills (1781-1855)

Westover, Virginia, *c.*1730

State House, Boston, 1793-98
Charles Bulfinch (1763-1844)

Redwood Library, Newport, Rhode
Island, 1750 *Peter Harrison (1716-75):*
born England; U.S.A. 1740

Temple, Nîmes

State House, Richmond,
Virginia, 1785-96 *Jefferson*

Trinity Church,
New York, 18.
Richard Upjo
(1802-1878

First
design

Monticello, Charlottesville
1770-1809
Thomas Jefferson (1743-1820); studied Roman buildings in Europe 1784-89

the Pantheon,
Rome

University of Virginia, Charlottesville, 1822-

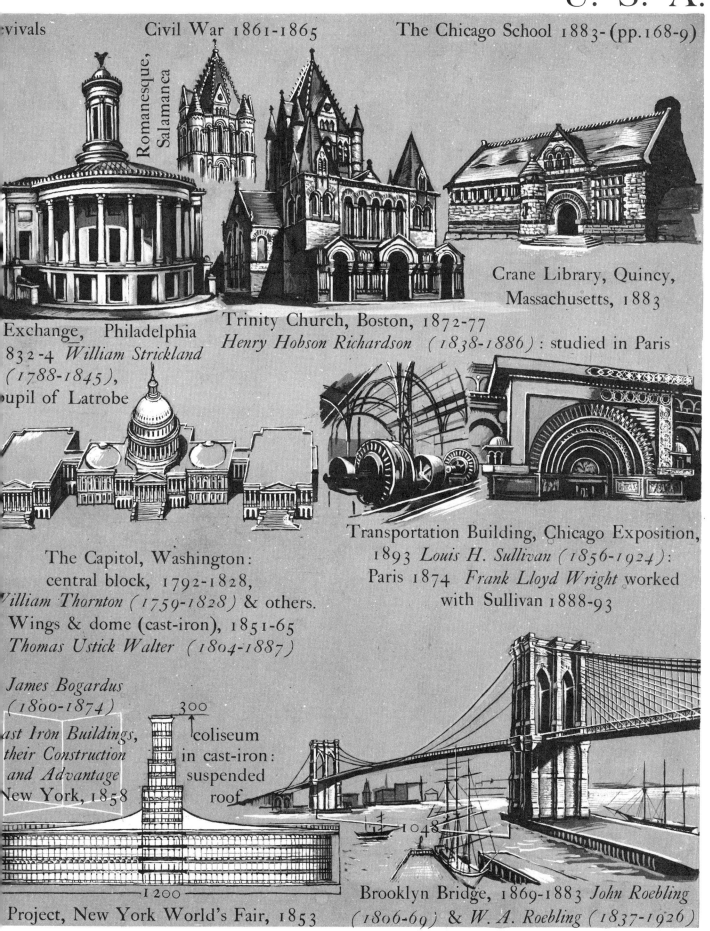

...vivals

Civil War 1861-1865

The Chicago School 1883- (pp.168-9)

Romanesque, Salamanca

Crane Library, Quincy, Massachusetts, 1883

...Exchange, Philadelphia 832-4 *William Strickland (1788-1845),* ...upil of Latrobe

Trinity Church, Boston, 1872-77
Henry Hobson Richardson (1838-1886) : studied in Paris

The Capitol, Washington:
central block, 1792-1828,
William Thornton (1759-1828) & others.
Wings & dome (cast-iron), 1851-65
Thomas Ustick Walter (1804-1887)

Transportation Building, Chicago Exposition,
1893 *Louis H. Sullivan (1856-1924)* :
Paris 1874 *Frank Lloyd Wright* worked
with Sullivan 1888-93

*James Bogardus
(1800-1874)
...ast Iron Buildings,
their Construction
and Advantage
New York,* 1858

300

coliseum
in cast-iron:
suspended
roof

1200

Project, New York World's Fair, 1853

Brooklyn Bridge, 1869-1883 *John Roebling
(1806-69)* & *W. A. Roebling (1837-1926)*

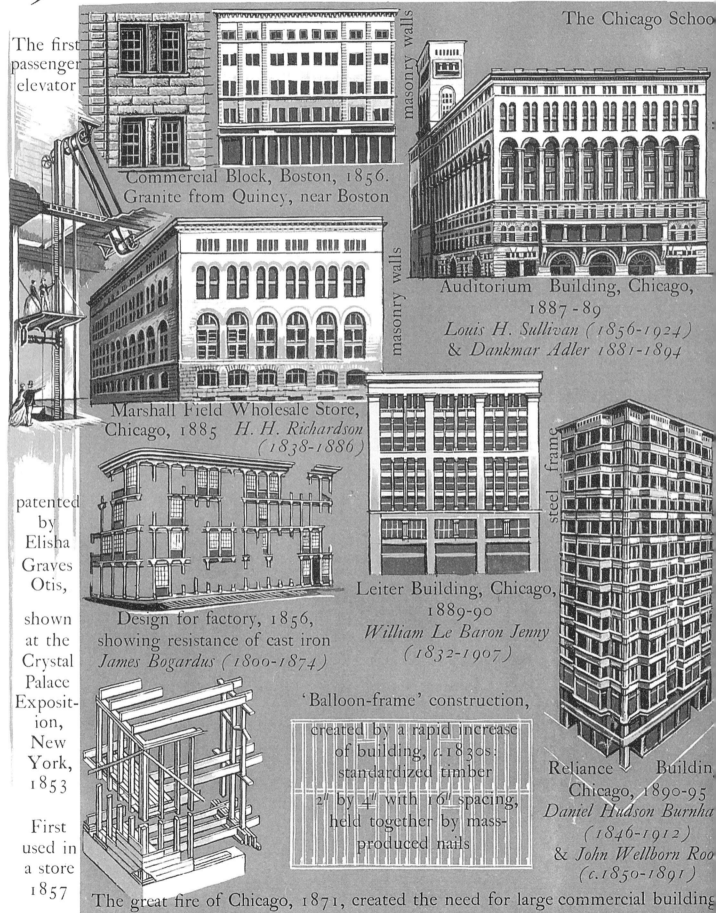

The Chicago School

The first passenger elevator

Commercial Block, Boston, 1856.
Granite from Quincy, near Boston

masonry walls

masonry walls

Auditorium Building, Chicago,
1887 - 89
Louis H. Sullivan (1856-1924)
& Dankmar Adler 1881-1894

Marshall Field Wholesale Store,
Chicago, 1885 *H. H. Richardson*
(1838-1886)

steel frame

patented
by
Elisha
Graves
Otis,

shown
at the
Crystal
Palace
Exposit-
ion,
New
York,
1853

First
used in
a store
1857

Design for factory, 1856,
showing resistance of cast iron
James Bogardus (1800-1874)

Leiter Building, Chicago,
1889-90
William Le Baron Jenny
(1832-1907)

'Balloon-frame' construction,
created by a rapid increase
of building, c.1830s:
standardized timber
2″ by 4″ with 16″ spacing,
held together by mass-
produced nails

Reliance   Buildin
Chicago, 1890-95
Daniel Hudson Burnha
(1846-1912)
& John Wellborn Roo
(c.1850-1891)

The great fire of Chicago, 1871, created the need for large commercial building

U. S. A. - THE SKYSCRAPER

19TH & 20TH CENTURIES

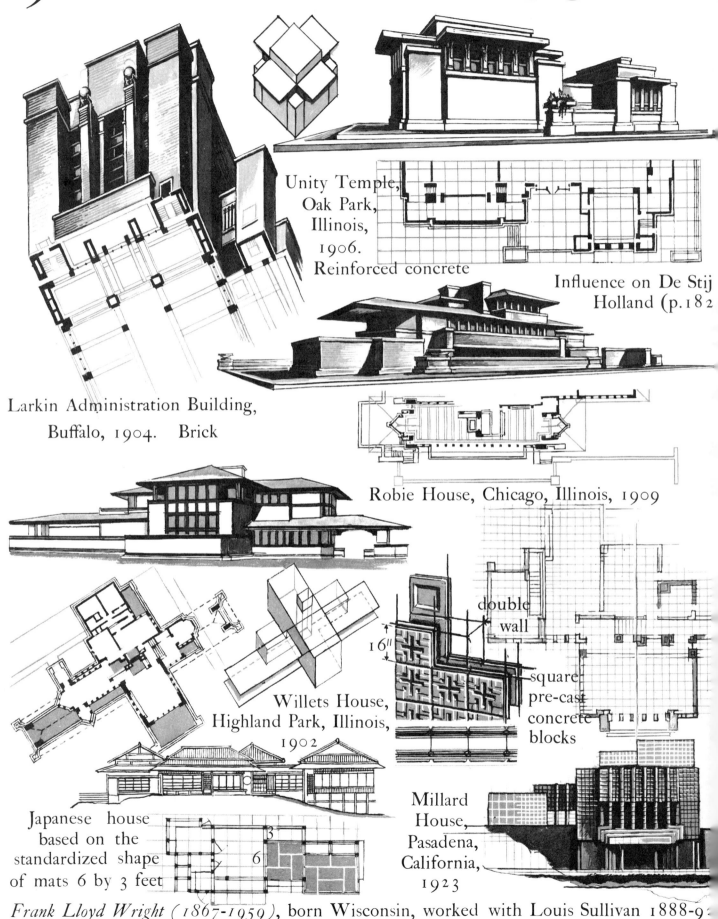

Unity Temple, Oak Park, Illinois, 1906. Reinforced concrete

Influence on De Stij Holland (p.182

Larkin Administration Building, Buffalo, 1904. Brick

Robie House, Chicago, Illinois, 1909

double wall

16"

square pre-cast concrete blocks

Willets House, Highland Park, Illinois, 1902

Japanese house based on the standardized shape of mats 6 by 3 feet

Millard House, Pasadena, California, 1923

Frank Lloyd Wright (1867-1959), born Wisconsin, worked with Louis Sullivan 1888-9

U.S.A., FRANK LLOYD WRIGHT

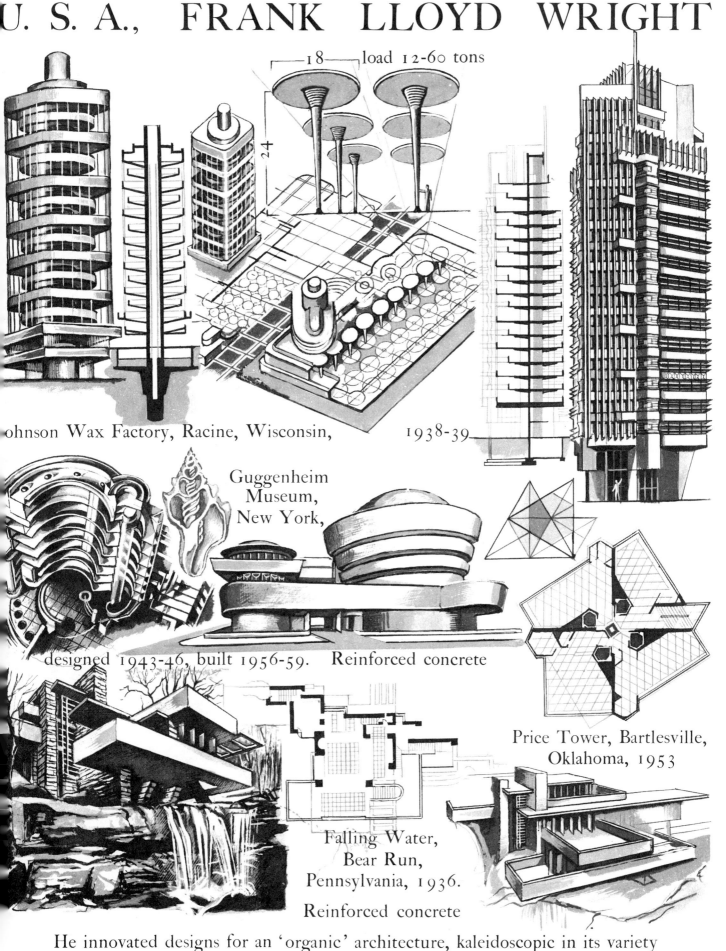

18 — load 12-60 tons

24

ohnson Wax Factory, Racine, Wisconsin, 1938-39

Guggenheim Museum, New York,

designed 1943-46, built 1956-59. Reinforced concrete

Price Tower, Bartlesville, Oklahoma, 1953

Falling Water, Bear Run, Pennsylvania, 1936. Reinforced concrete

He innovated designs for an 'organic' architecture, kaleidoscopic in its variety

Project: National Theatre, Berlin, 1800
Frederick Gilly (1771-1800)

Studies in proportions, 1898
Endell

Altes Museum, Berlin, 1824-28 *Schinkel*

Schloss Linderhof, nr Oberammergau, 1870-86 *Georg von Dollman (1830-95)*

Elvira Photographic Studio, *August Endell (1871-1925)*

5O

5O

Schauspielhaus, Berlin, 1819-21
Karl Friedrich Von Schinkel (1781-1841)

The Propylaeon, Munich, 1846-63 *Leo von Klenze (1784-1864)*

Wertheim Store, Berlin, 1896 *A. Messel (1853-1909)*

| J.-N.-L. Durand (1760-1834) *Précis des Leçons d'Architecture données à l'École Polytechnique Paris, 1802-05* | rational designs for Greek, Roman, Early Christian & Romanesque architecture | Classical-Romantic moods generated by *Winklemann (1717-1768) Lessing (1729-1781) Goethe (1749-1832) Heine (1797-1856)* | Art Nouveau, 1890-191 Germany: *Jugendstil* France: *style nouille* (noodle style) or *style Guimard* Italy: *stile Liberty* (after the London shop or *stile floreale* Spain: *modernismo* |

steel frame

steel hinge A

load

loading and deflection

rein-forced concrete

bending moments

concrete A

A.E.G. Turbine Factory, Berlin, 1909 *Peter Behrens (1868-1940):*

3-hinged steel frame

8o

Foundry, Kattowitz, 1910 2-hinged frame

director of School of Art, Dusseldorf, 1903-07. In 1907, the year the Deutscher Werkbund was founded as a centre for artists, architects & industrialists, Behrens was appointed designer to the A.E.G. (German General Electric Company). *Gropius* worked under Behrens 1907-10, *Mies van der Rohe* 1908-11, & *Le Corbusier* 1910-11

3-hinged frames

Jahrhunderthalle, Breslau, 1910-12 reinforced concrete *Max Berg (1870-)*

brick faced with concrete.

chool of Art, Weimar, 1906 *Henry van de Velde (1863-957):* born Antwerp, organised the Weimar School of Art, 906-14 (which re-opened 1919 under *Gropius* as the Bauhaus)

Einstein Tower, Potsdam, 1920-21. *Eric Mendelsohn (1887-1953):* England and Palestine 1933-41; U.S.A. from 1941

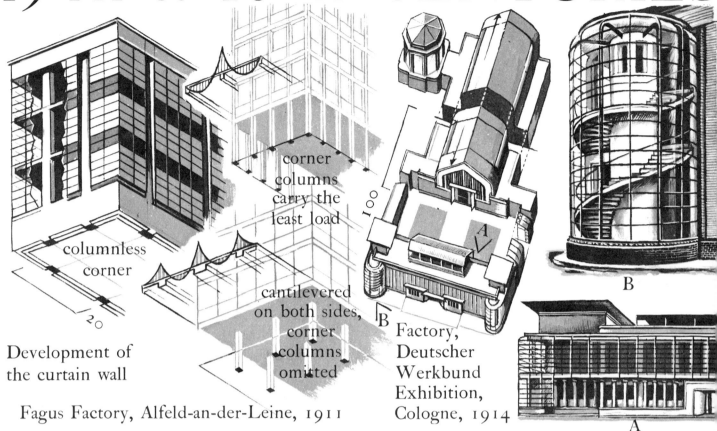

columnless corner

20

corner columns carry the least load

cantilevered on both sides, corner columns omitted

Development of the curtain wall

Factory, Deutscher Werkbund Exhibition, Cologne, 1914

B

A

Fagus Factory, Alfeld-an-der-Leine, 1911

Walter Gropius (1883-): assistant to Behrens, 1907-11 (p.173); director of the Bauhaus,

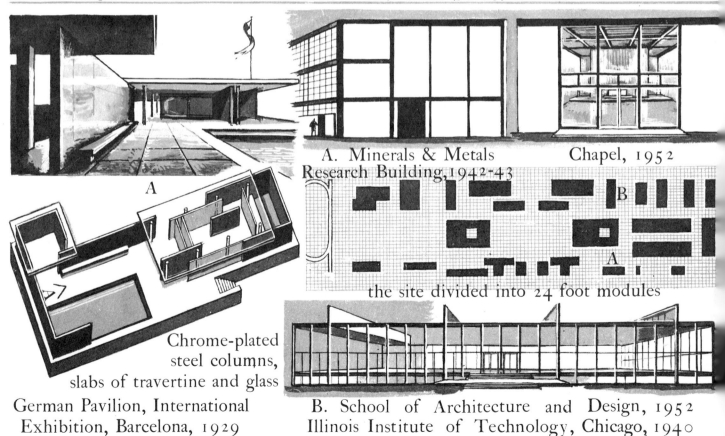

A

A. Minerals & Metals Research Building, 1942-43

Chapel, 1952

B

A

the site divided into 24 foot modules

Chrome-plated steel columns, slabs of travertine and glass

German Pavilion, International Exhibition, Barcelona, 1929

B. School of Architecture and Design, 1952 Illinois Institute of Technology, Chicago, 1940

Ludwig Mies van der Rohe (1886-): born Aachen, Germany; worked with Behrens 1908-1

GERMANY & U.S.A.

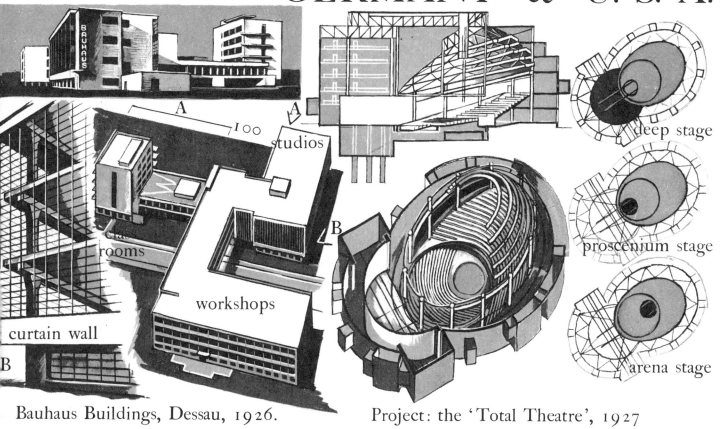

deep stage

proscenium stage

arena stage

Bauhaus Buildings, Dessau, 1926.   Project: the 'Total Theatre', 1927

Weimar 1919-25, at Dessau 1925-8; worked in England 1934-37 (p.161), U.S.A. 1937

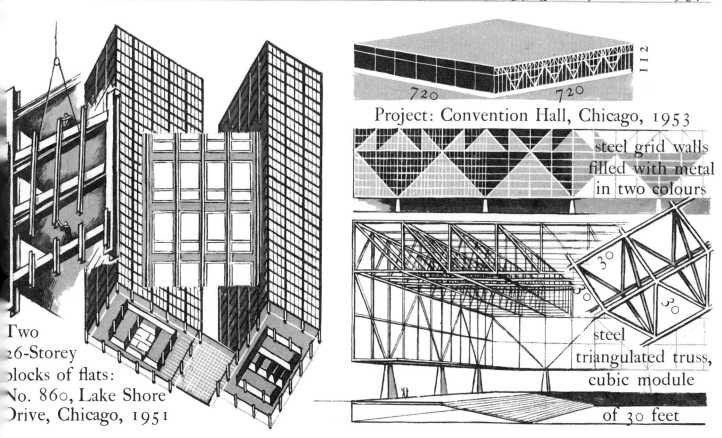

Project: Convention Hall, Chicago, 1953

steel grid walls filled with metal in two colours

steel triangulated truss, cubic module of 30 feet

Two 26-Storey blocks of flats: No. 860, Lake Shore Drive, Chicago, 1951

director of the Bauhaus, Dessau, 1930-33; to U.S.A., 1937. His dictum: 'less is more'

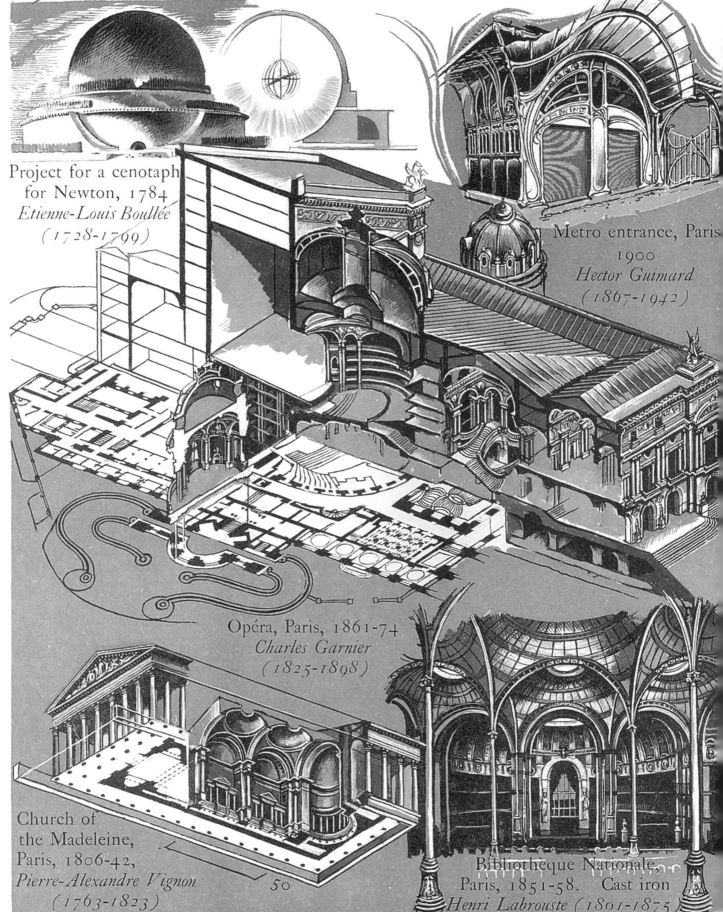

19TH & 20TH CENTURIES

Project for a cenotaph
for Newton, 1784
Etienne-Louis Boullée
(1728-1799)

Metro entrance, Paris
1900
Hector Guimard
(1867-1942)

Opéra, Paris, 1861-74
Charles Garnier
(1825-1898)

Church of
the Madeleine,
Paris, 1806-42,
Pierre-Alexandre Vignon
(1763-1823)

50

Bibliothèque Nationale,
Paris, 1851-58.   Cast iron
Henri Labrouste (1801-1875)

FRANCE

S. Jean de Montmartre, Paris, 1894: first church in reinforced concrete *Anatole de Baudot (1834-1915)*

pre-cast, glazed concrete elements

50

Eiffel developed space frames & aero-dynamics

wind

Notre-Dame du Raincy, Paris, 1922-23. Exposed concrete, barrel-vaulted roof, less than 2" at apex, carried on reinforced concrete columns *Auguste Perret:* Le Corbusier worked with him 1908

50

Eiffel Tower, Paris, 1889. Wrought iron *Eiffel*

3.67 556

hinged joint

Truyère Bridge, nr Aurillac, France, 1880-84 *Gustave Eiffel (1832-1923)*

Flats, Rue Franklin, Paris, 1903. Exposed reinforced concrete framework *Auguste Perret (1874-1954)*

177

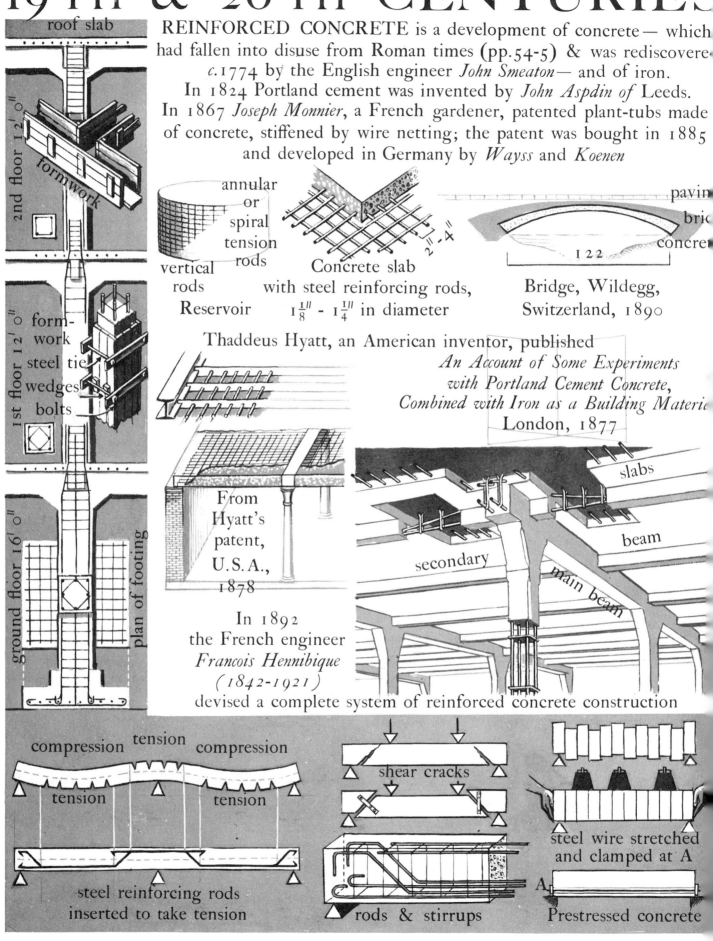

19TH & 20TH CENTURIES

roof slab

2nd floor 12' 0"

formwork

1st floor 12' 0"

form-work
steel tie
wedges
bolts

ground floor 16' 0"

plan of footing

REINFORCED CONCRETE is a development of concrete — which had fallen into disuse from Roman times (pp.54-5) & was rediscovered c.1774 by the English engineer *John Smeaton* — and of iron.
In 1824 Portland cement was invented by *John Aspdin of* Leeds.
In 1867 *Joseph Monnier*, a French gardener, patented plant-tubs made of concrete, stiffened by wire netting; the patent was bought in 1885 and developed in Germany by *Wayss* and *Koenen*

annular
or
spiral
tension
rods
vertical
rods

Reservoir

Concrete slab
with steel reinforcing rods,
$1\frac{1}{8}$" - $1\frac{1}{4}$" in diameter

2"-4"

paving
brick
concrete

1 2 2

Bridge, Wildegg,
Switzerland, 1890

Thaddeus Hyatt, an American inventor, published
*An Account of Some Experiments
with Portland Cement Concrete,
Combined with Iron as a Building Material*
London, 1877

From
Hyatt's
patent,
U.S.A.,
1878

In 1892
the French engineer
*Francois Hennibique
(1842-1921)*
devised a complete system of reinforced concrete construction

slabs

beam

secondary

main beam

compression   tension   compression

tension   tension

steel reinforcing rods
inserted to take tension

shear cracks

rods & stirrups

steel wire stretched
and clamped at A

A

Prestressed concrete

REINFORCED CONCRETE

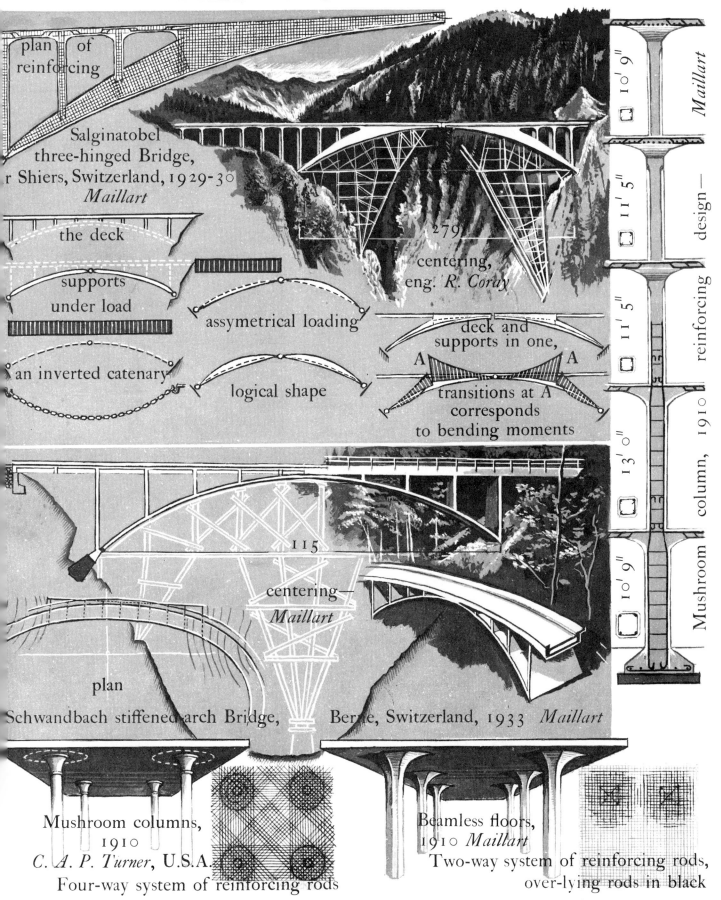

plan of reinforcing

Salginatobel three-hinged Bridge, r Shiers, Switzerland, 1929-30 *Maillart*

the deck

supports under load

assymetrical loading

an inverted catenary

logical shape

279

centering, eng. *R. Coray*

deck and supports in one,
A   A
transitions at A corresponds to bending moments

115

centering—
Maillart

plan

Schwandbach stiffened arch Bridge, Berne, Switzerland, 1933 *Maillart*

Maillart

10' 9"

11' 5"

11' 5"

13' 0"

10' 9"

reinforcing design—

Mushroom column, 1910

Mushroom columns,
1910
C. A. P. Turner, U.S.A.
Four-way system of reinforcing rods

Beamless floors,
1910 *Maillart*
Two-way system of reinforcing rods,
over-lying rods in black

Robert Maillart (1872-1940), born Berne, Switzerland, engineer in reinforced concrete

19 TH & 20 TH CENTURIES

Le Corbusier (Charles-Edouard Jeanneret)
(1887-1965), painter, architect, writer and theorist,
born Chaux-de-Fonds, Switzerland. Learnt the
use of reinforced concrete from *Perret* in Paris,
1908, worked under *Behrens*, with *Gropius* and
Mies van der Rohe, in Berlin, 1910.

Vers une Architecture,
Paris, 1923
Urbanisme, 1925
La Ville Radieuse, 1935
The Modulor, 1949
La Poeme de l'Angle Droit,
1955, and other works

As a 'cubist' painter,
in 1918, with *Ozenfant*,
he founded 'Purism'

and a review,
L'Esprit Nouveau

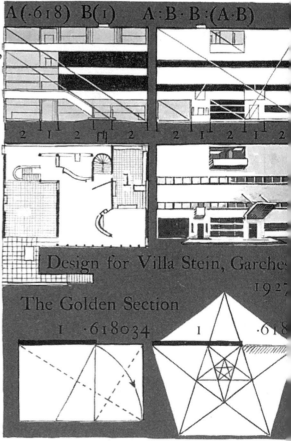

Design for Villa Stein, Garches
1927

The Golden Section
1 ·618034   1   ·618

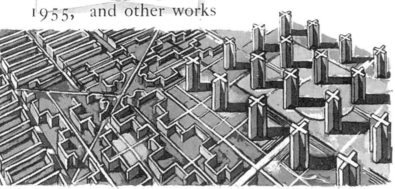

Contemporary city of three million inhabitants
From *Vers une Architecture*, Paris, 1923

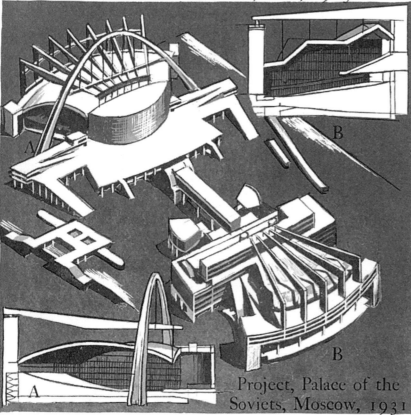

A
B
B

Project, Palace of the
Soviets, Moscow, 1931

'The Modulor a harmonious measure
to the Human Scale....& the Cosm
Orders.'

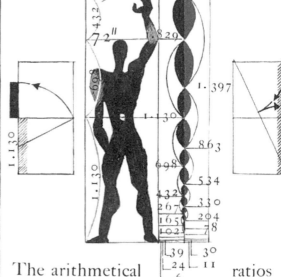

The arithmetical   ratios
follow the   series of
Fibonnaci of Pisa (b. 1175):
$1, (1+1)2, (2+1)3, (3+2)5, (5+3)8$.
$\frac{1}{1} + \circ, \frac{2}{1} = 2 \cdot \circ, \frac{3}{2} = 1 \cdot 5, \frac{5}{3} = 1 \cdot 66, \frac{8}{5} = 1 \cdot 6$.
that is they approach nearer and nea
to the Golden Section, 1·618034

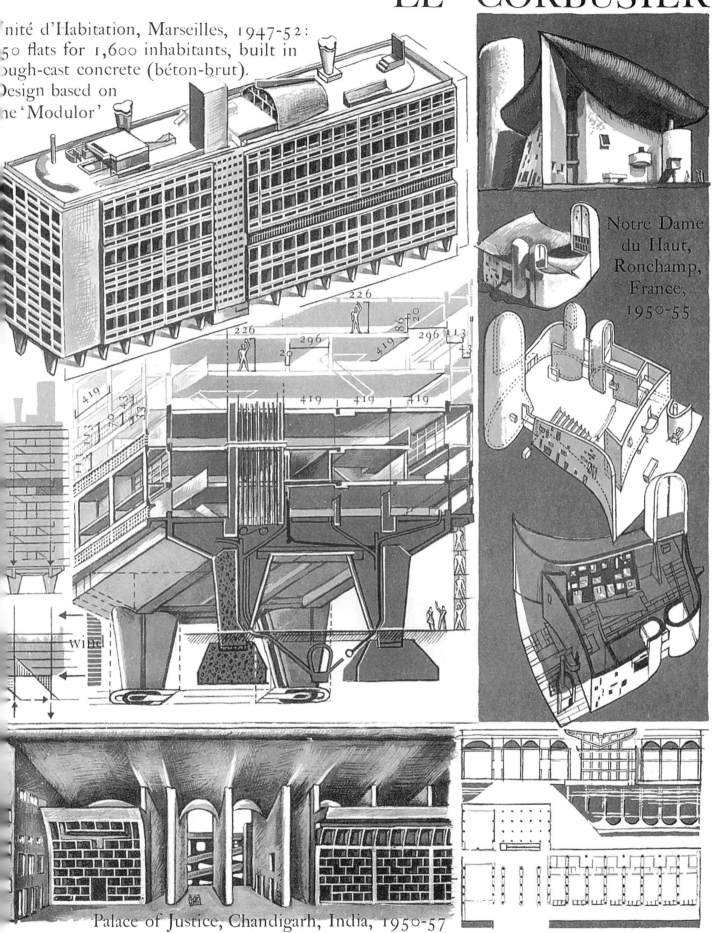

LE CORBUSIER

Unité d'Habitation, Marseilles, 1947-52:
350 flats for 1,600 inhabitants, built in
rough-cast concrete (béton-brut).
Design based on
the 'Modulor'

Notre Dame
du Haut,
Ronchamp,
France,
1950-55

wind

Palace of Justice, Chandigarh, India, 1950-57

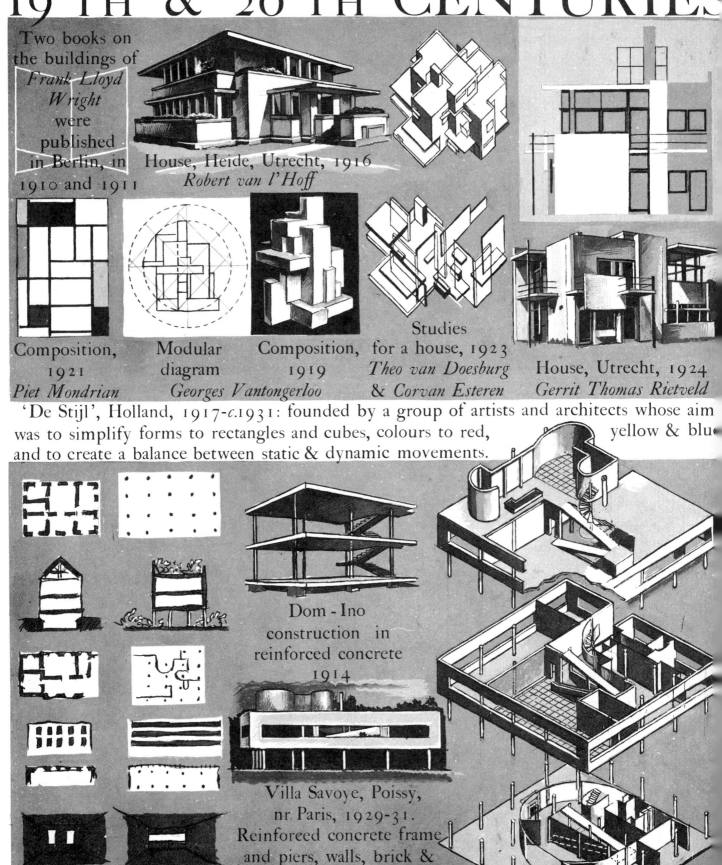

Two books on the buildings of *Frank Lloyd Wright* were published in Berlin, in 1910 and 1911

House, Heide, Utrecht, 1916
Robert van l'Hoff

Composition, 1921
Piet Mondrian

Modular diagram
Georges Vantongerloo

Composition, 1919

Studies for a house, 1923
Theo van Doesburg & Cor van Esteren

House, Utrecht, 1924
Gerrit Thomas Rietveld

'De Stijl', Holland, 1917-c.1931: founded by a group of artists and architects whose aim was to simplify forms to rectangles and cubes, colours to red, yellow & blue, and to create a balance between static & dynamic movements.

Dom-Ino construction in reinforced concrete 1914

Villa Savoye, Poissy, nr. Paris, 1929-31. Reinforced concrete frame and piers, walls, brick & breeze blocks, floors and roof, hollow tiles.

traditional   new
Five points of view

Le Corbusier (1877-1965) (pp.180-1)

THE MODERN HOUSE

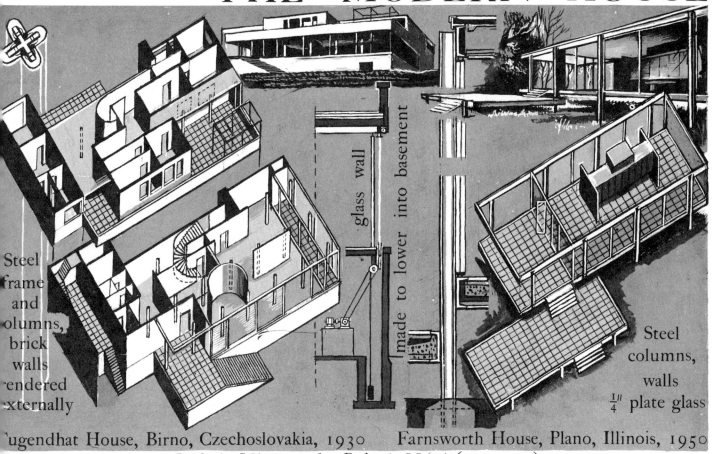

Steel frame and columns, brick walls rendered externally

glass wall | made to lower into basement

Steel columns, walls $\frac{1''}{4}$ plate glass

Tugendhat House, Birno, Czechoslovakia, 1930   Farnsworth House, Plano, Illinois, 1950

Ludwig Mies van der Rohe (1886-) (pp.174-5)

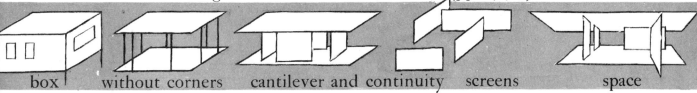

box   without corners   cantilever and continuity   screens   space

Diagrams from Frank Lloyd Wright *The Destruction of the Box*

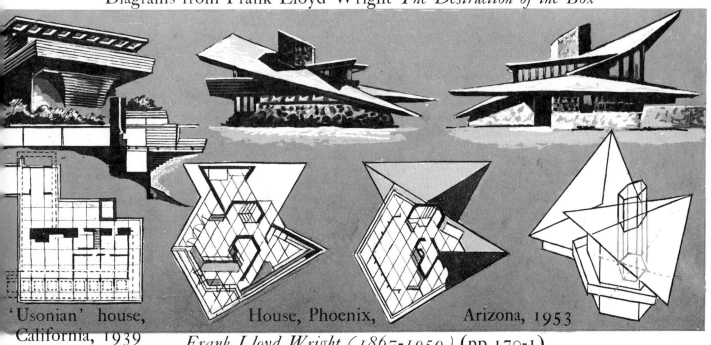

'Usonian' house, California, 1939   House, Phoenix,   Arizona, 1953

Frank Lloyd Wright (1867-1959) (pp.170-1)

Municipal Stadium,
Florence, 1930-32
Nervi

20

50

stairway to grandstand

stages ... in the ... design

Lamella roof

principal ... stress lines

131

328

detail of
Hangar, nr Rome, 1935 *Nervi*

Hangar, Orvieto,
1940
Versions built at
Orbetello &
Torre del Lago,
1935-41

wind ... wind

Peri Luigi Nervi (1891-), born Lombardy, engineer in reinforced concrete, follows 'bo

Corrugated roof composed of prefabricated units 13' 0" long 1½" thick joined at A by concrete poured *in situ*

8' 2"

33°

ferro-cemento
fine steel mesh 0.02"–0.06" sprayed with mortar cement

2'

concrete

Section of joints of prefabricated units 13' 0" by 6' 6" & ¾" thick

Exhibition Hall, Turin, 1948-50 — *Nervi* developed prefabricated units of *ferro-cemento* (iron-concrete), speedily assembled on a light scaffolding

100

Palazzetto dello Sport, Rome, 1956-57
Arch. *Annibale Vitellozzi*, eng. *Nervi*

e intuitive & mathematical paths'.   Author of *Construction, Science or Art?*, Rome, 1945

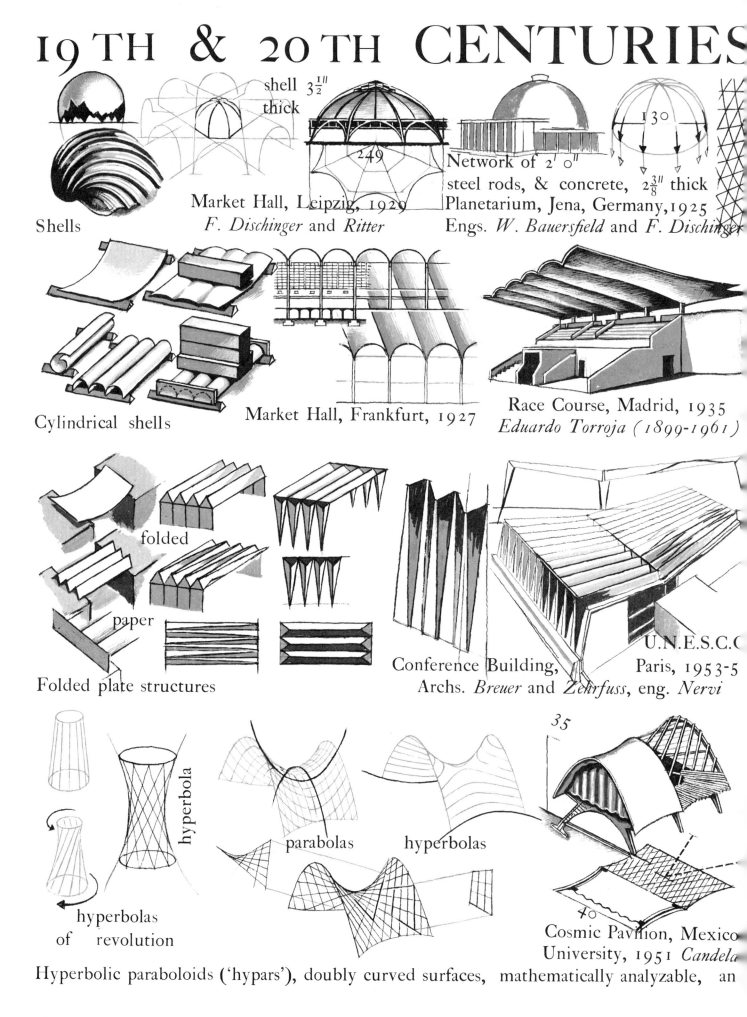

shell $3\frac{1}{2}''$ thick

249

Market Hall, Leipzig, 1929
F. Dischinger and *Ritter*

Network of 2′ 0″ steel rods, & concrete, $2\frac{3}{8}''$ thick

130

Planetarium, Jena, Germany, 1925
Engs. *W. Bauersfield* and *F. Dischinger*

Shells

Cylindrical shells

Market Hall, Frankfurt, 1927

Race Course, Madrid, 1935
Eduardo Torroja (1899-1961)

folded

paper

Folded plate structures

Conference Building, U.N.E.S.C.O. Paris, 1953-5
Archs. *Breuer* and *Zehrfuss*, eng. *Nervi*

hyperbola

hyperbolas of revolution

parabolas

hyperbolas

35

40

Cosmic Pavilion, Mexico University, 1951 *Candela*

Hyperbolic paraboloids ('hypars'), doubly curved surfaces, mathematically analyzable, an

SHELL CONCRETE

Formwork & reinforcing rods, sprayed with Portland cement concrete, $2\frac{3}{8}''$ thick: Cement Hall, Swiss Exhibition, Zurich, 1938 *R. Maillart (1872-1940)*

7°
39'
53

Collegiate Church, St Louis Archs. *Helmuth, Obata* and *Kassobaum,* eng. *Nervi*

255

double shell
$2\frac{1}{2}''$
$2\frac{1}{2}''$
5' 8''
158'
38

C.N.I.T. Exhibition Hall, Paris, 1958 *Camelot, De Mailly* and *Zehrfuss*

88

Notre Dame de Royan, France, 1954-59 Archs. *G. Gillet, B. Laffaile* and *R. Sager*

From a model for the Cathedral, Brazilia, 1960 *Oscar Niemeyer (1907-)*

30°

Exchange Hall, Mexico, 1955 *E. de la Mora* & *F. L. Carmona*

Project for Cathedral, Australia *A. Nervi* and *C. Vannoni*

Philips Pavilion, Brussels, 1958 *Le Corbusier*

easy to build with formwork of straight planks, largely developed by *Candela* (pp. 188-9)

$\frac{3}{4}''$ rods

$\frac{3}{8}''$ rods

$\frac{1}{2}''$ rods

'Hypar' umbrella, 1952 *Candela*

'Hypar' umbrella warehouse: Linda Vista, Mexico, 1954 *Candela*

derivation of the form of the roof

column

Church of the Miraculous Virgin, Narvarte, Mexico, 1954-55 *Candela*

El Altillo Chapel, Coyoscan, Mexico, 1955
Candela, Enrique de la Mora and *Fernando Lopez Carmona*

Felix Candela (1910-): born and studied at Madrid, Mexico 1939 onwards.   Since 1951

Church, Monterrey, Nuevo León, Mexico, 1959

Candela, Enrique de la Mora and Fernando Lopez Carmona

5°

5°

5°

Chapel, Morelos, Mexico, 1958-59

Candela, Guillermo Rosell and Manuel Larrosa

Restaurant, Xochimilco, Mexico, 1957-58 *Candela*

5°

formwork

...e has developed the hyperbolic paraboloid ('hypar'), often working with other architects

T. W. A. Terminal, Kennedy Air Port, New York, 1956-62
Eero Saarinen (1910-61), born Finland, went to U.S.A. in 1923

sphere   tetrahedron   octahedron

icosahedron

strut

gusset

hub

Union Dome, Baton Rouge, Louisiana, 1958-59.
steel panels, each folded
with tubes & rods

321 hexago
and brac

145

geodosic
grid

Kaiser Aluminium Dome, Hawaii, 1957. Erected in 22 ho
Geodosic Domes from 1948 *Richard Buckminster Fuller (1895-)*, 'comprehensive design

384

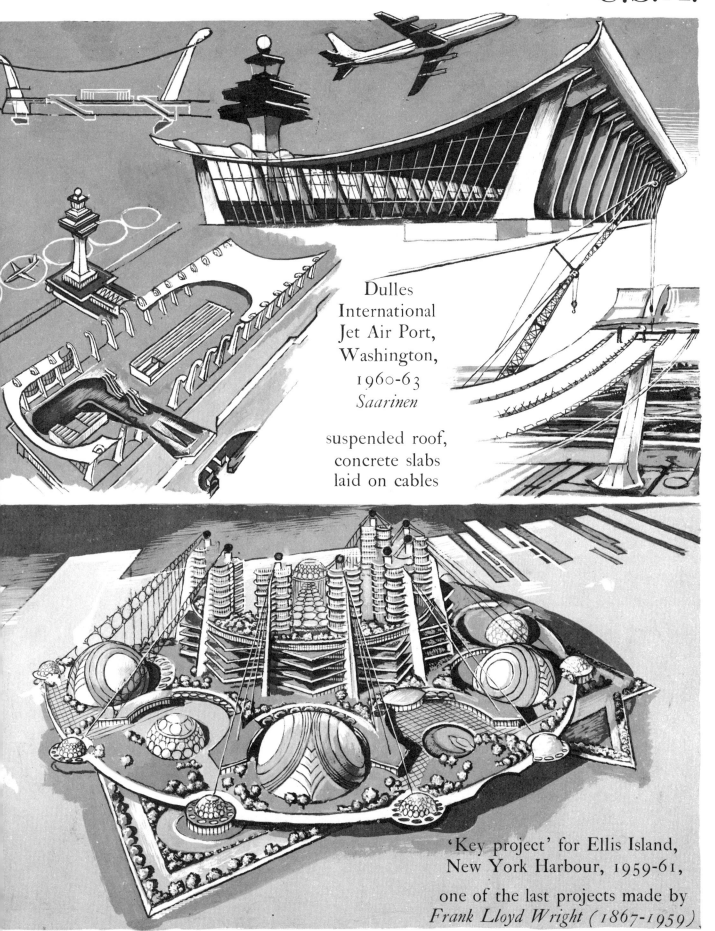

Dulles
International
Jet Air Port,
Washington,
1960-63
Saarinen

suspended roof,
concrete slabs
laid on cables

'Key project' for Ellis Island,
New York Harbour, 1959-61,

one of the last projects made by
Frank Lloyd Wright (1867-1959)

Short Bibliography

Note—More extensive bibliographies can be found in the books
marked below with an asterisk

General

CHOISY, A. *Histoire de l'Architecture*, Paris 1899; reprinted 1964 (for drawings)

FLETCHER, SIR BANISTER *A History of Architecture on the Comparative Method*, B. T. Batsford Ltd., 1896; The Athlone Press, 1960*

GIEDON, S. *Space, Time and Architecture*, Oxford University Press, 1950 4th ed. 1962

LAVEDAN, P. *French Architecture*, Penguin Books Ltd., 1956

PEVSNER, N. *An Outline of European Architecture*, Penguin Books Ltd., 1943, 7th edition, new format 1963*

STATHAM, H. H. Revised H. Braun, *A History of Architecture*, B. T. Batsford Ltd., 1950

YARWOOD, D. *The Architecture of England*, B. T. Batsford Ltd., 1963

Proportion

HAMBIDGE, J. *The Parthenon and other Greek Temples. Their Dynamic Symmetry*, Newhaven, 1924

LE CORBUSIER, *The Modulor*, Faber and Faber Ltd., 1954

SCHOLFIELD, P. M. *The Theory of Proportion in Architecture*, Cambridge University Press, 1958*

WITTKOWER, R. *Architectural Principles in the Age of Humanism*, Alec Tiranti Ltd., 1952

Egypt and Western Asia

EDWARDS, I. E. S. *The Pyramids of Egypt*, Penguin Books Ltd., 1955

STEVENSON SMITH, W. *The Art and Architecture of Ancient Egypt* (Pelican History of Art), Penguin Books Ltd., 1958*

FRANKFORT, H. *The Art and Architecture of the Ancient Orient* (Pelican History of Art), Penguin Books Ltd., 1954*

Greek and Roman

DINSMOOR, W. B. *The Architecture of Ancient Greece*, B. T. Batsford Ltd., 1927

LAWRENCE, A. W. *Greek Architecture* (Pelican History of Art), Penguin Books Ltd., 1957*

STEWART, C. *Ancient and Classical Architecture* (new edition, Simpson's History of Architectural Development), London

ROBERTSON, D. S. *Greek and Roman Architecture*, Cambridge University Press, 1943

VITRUVIUS, *The Ten Books on Architecture* (Translated by M. H. Morgan), New York, 1960

Early Christian, Byzantine and Romanesque

CONANT, K. J. *Carolingian and Romanesque Architecture, 800-1200* (Pelican History of Art), Penguin Books Ltd., 1959*

STEWART, C. *Early Christian, Byzantine and Romanesque Architecture* (new edition, Simpson's History of Architectural development), Longman's, Green & Co., 1954

Gothic

ADAMS, H. *Mont-Saint-Michel and Chartres*, New York, 1961

FRANKL, P. *Gothic Architecture* (Pelican History of Art), Penguin Books Ltd., 1963*

GIMPEL, J. *The Cathedral Builders*, New York, London, 1961

WEBB, G. *Architecture in Britain: The Middle Ages* (Pelican History of Art), Penguin Books Ltd., 1955

Renaissance — Baroque

FOKKER, T. H. *Roman Baroque Art*, 2 vols, Oxford University Press, 1938

HUGHES, J. Q. & LYNTON, N. *Renaissance Architecture*, Prentice Hall International Inc. (new edition, Simpson's History of Architectural Development), 1962

WOLFFLIN, H. *Renaissance and Baroque*, Wm. Collins, Sons Ltd., 1964

Italy
WITTKOWER, R. *Art and Architecture in Italy 1600-1750*, Penguin Books Ltd., 1958*

England
SUMMERSON, J. *Architecture in Britain 1530-1830*, Penguin Books Ltd., 1958*

France
BLUNT, A. *Art and Architecture in France 1500-1700*, Penguin Books Ltd., 1953*

Spain
KUBLER, G. and Soria, M. S. *Art and Architecture in Spain and Portugal, and their American Dominions 1500-1800*, Penguin Books Ltd., 1959*

These four volumes form part of the Pelican History of Art

Nineteenth and Twentieth Centuries

HITCHCOCK, H. R. *Architecture: Nineteenth and Twentieth Centuries* (Pelican History of Art), Penguin Books Ltd., 1963*

BANHAM, R. *Theory and Design in the First Machine Age*, Architectural Press Ltd., 1960

JOEDICKE, J. A. *A History of Modern Architecture*, New York, London, 1959

SIEGEL, C. *Structure and Form in Modern Architecture*, New York, London, 1962